MW00939851

Transformed

for

Purpose

A Practical Plan To Get Unstuck And

Live A Power-Filled Life

Andrea Humphrey

Table of Contents

Acknowledgments

The transformation journey you are about to embark upon is in large part due to Ms. Nikki Woods who pushed me to turn a 30-day journal into a full book. Thank you, Nikki, for believing that this book could be, thank you for believing in me.

As always, thank you to my incredible husband Charles, who always allows me to dream and to fly, causing our lives to constantly transform with each endeavor God brings my way. To my beautiful daughters Lauryn and Sydney, you teach and inspire me daily, watching you is a constant reminder that change is forever a part of our lives and that it is *good*. I love the two of you so dearly and I love the amazing young women you are becoming. I thank God for entrusting me with you and I am so proud to be your mom.

Tonee, thank you for being a great son to me. I am so very proud of you! Devon, thank you for making me better and helping me push forward with the call on my life. Don, you are brilliant and I am so grateful God blessed me with you.

Chante' (Thelma) ~ To borrow a line from Glinda and Elphaba, "Who can say if I've been changed for the better? I believe I've been changed for the better. Because I knew you I've been changed for the good" (RoD). Cheryl, thank you for always re-minding me that there is more in me. Thank you for the pocket note! Eman, I love you. Dr. Henry, you have no idea how much you inspire me! I am grateful for your friendship. Michelle C., Thank you for help-ing me with self-care.

Pastors - Brooks, Tyran, Jon and Tate, you are true brothers to me and you make my imagination come alive!

Jonathan Sprinkles, in one hour you gave me more confidence than most have in a year. Over the "Hump" I go!

To my parents & Godparents, siblings and extended family, I love you and thank God for His grace in our lives.

Hope's House (including but not limited to: Kelvin, Iris, Rae, Ese, Chris, Tish, Lynn, Nina, Marc2, Tiffany, Tracey, Stacy, Eric & Sekou) you are the best church I know and I am honored to be a part of what God is doing in the world through us.

Kidd Marketing thanks for your professionalism and for delivering on your promise!

This book is dedicated to the memory of Dr. Sharon Rabb who helped transform my heart, my mind and my life by just being. I miss you more than words could ever express. Thank you for loving me enough to challenge me to transform how I see my-self.

I thank God that when it looked like the plan of God was fading into the horizon, never to come to fruition, He reached down with His incredible hand of Grace and pulled me close and said... "I know the plan and the way, your change has come to-day!" Thank you God for your incredible, saving love.

Introducing

The Transformation That

Is Coming in Your Life!

Transformation is coming! Transformation is coming! Real, authentic, powerful change that is effective, purposeful and lasting is coming. The fact that you are reading this book tells me you are looking for it. You desire it, you want it and somewhere deep inside you, you believe it is possible. I, too, believe you will have what you declare and go after if it is purposeful for your life *and* in the mind of your Creator. You do have a purpose. You know that, right? Before the world was formed there was a planned purpose for your existence. In fact, Jeremiah 1:5 says: "Before I formed you in the womb I knew you, before you were born I set you apart..." That is incredibly good news. You are not here by happenstance!

My friend, God had a purpose for all of us before we were ever born. Many of us never seek to know it. For those who have tapped into that purpose, life has a way of fulfilling itself and transforming our ordinary, mediocre and even wayward lives into adventures that are filled with joy, peace and gifts that reward us eternally. Now, please don't get me wrong, even when we know our purpose sometimes we all get off track for positive and not-so-positive reasons. From time to time, some of us are like kids who veer off into areas of life that perhaps well-meaning others have determined are good directions for us. Others of us are following the plan our parents had for themselves but did not accomplish and so they made them our plans. Still others have adopted the life, mission and personality of that which looked like it would garner the most money, attention, fame or whatever you deemed important to obtain.

In truth, you are happiest when you are fulfilling the purpose for which you were created. You are most at peace when you are able to be the authentic you that you were intended to be. When we are whole and passionate about life and operating in our purpose it only makes sense that we are then powerful! When we don't understand our purpose we have a tendency to abuse our lives and aimlessly wander around wasting time.

The purpose of this book is to walk you through 30 "power moves" in your personal life that will bring about emotional, physical, spiritual and mental transformation! I call them power moves because if you work on these areas, I believe you will become more powerful because you will be moving in your purpose. One of the best ways to become more effective is to look at your life and make adjustments according to your purpose in life. You will be amazed to see that even the smallest change can yield a huge harvest.

The world is waiting for what is inside of you. Perhaps you have noticed that our world is slowly slipping into a fragmented, divided and lonely place where many feel abandoned and without hope. You know that you have the ability to help make a difference but there are a few areas that slow you down and prevent you from walking in power. Today is the day that you begin to shift into a place of power by working on you so that you can be of better use to those around you. A better you means a better marriage, a better work environment, a better family, a better community and a better atmosphere wherever you are. Today, you launch into your transformation of finding purpose on purpose.

This book has a partner e-journal available online at www.andreahumphrey.com that serves to help you put into action the 30 areas we will work on to jump start a brand new direction in your life. Whether you are using it to pull yourself out of a temporary funk, make a dramatic course change in life or to simply refresh your heart and mind, these 30 transformation principals will remind you how powerful you really are and prayerfully push you to be the best you that you can be.

No matter what life stage you are in, there is a section that will be useful in challenging your thinking and behaviors, causing you to reflect and recalibrate so that the end result will be a better and more effective you.

I urge you to read through the book with a friend or two. Accountability has a lot of value. Ecclesiastes 4:9-12 says: "Two are better than one, because they have a good reward for their toil. For if they fall, one will lift up his fellow. But woe to him who is alone when he falls and has not another to lift him up! Again, if two lie together, they keep warm, but how can one keep warm alone? And though a man might prevail against one who is alone, two will withstand him—a threefold cord is not quickly broken."

There is a reason that so many people lose weight with Weight Watchers. Simply having someone check on you makes a big difference. So get a partner and make it work for the two of you. Take a chance and be vulnerable and transparent. Show your heart and make it a point to see your partner's as well. Push one another to grow and follow through on what each section of the journal is asking of you.

Use the 30-Day Transformation Journal to chart your growth and see how your Creator is working in your life.

I wish you well on this journey. I know you will enjoy the process and will come away better. With growth there is sometimes pain, but I promise that if you keep working through it, it will be worth the discomfort. I look forward to hearing your stories of transformation and I pray that we will meet someday. We can all be made better by sharing about the goodness derived from the transformation process.

Until then, know that you have been prayed for today! Let's go!

Mindset Reset!

So I was running (well actually fast walking) with my trainer the other day and she started telling me this story about how her ex-husband had recently called her to tell her how he had remarried on Halloween day. With a voice that spoke of her complete and utter disbelief, she relayed the story about how he got married in, of all things, a Batman costume. And if this wasn't bad enough, his loving and doting bride stood at the altar in a corresponding Batgirl costume! Just in case I didn't believe her story, she pulled out her phone and began showing me what appears to be a true Facebook picture post of a man and woman standing at a makeshift altar with what looks like a preacher between them with a Bible in hand. There, in front of him, is an

African-American Batman and Batgirl holding hands, gazing lovingly into one another's eyes apparently saying "I do."

In my head I heard the theme music from the Batman movie! I was suddenly jerked back from my amused view of this photograph by my friend's high-pitched voice telling me about these trick-or-treat antics put on by her ex-husband. Just so you get the complete picture, she is describing, with some very colorful adjectives I might add, details about her ex-husband and telling me how crazy he is while frequently asking, "What kind of woman would marry this man?" and "Who would do it in a Batman costume on Halloween nonetheless?" She is going on and on about how ridiculous it is, and how it makes no sense for any woman at any given time to marry somebody who would have the nerve to marry you on Halloween in costume, without a ring, in a mask, playing the role of someone who already lived a double life in their movie life! On and on she went describing how crazy this was and how somebody had to be crazy in *their* mind to be with this man.

It was about the third iteration of that line in her story when it dawned on me that I should probably interrupt her because after all, this was *her* ex-husband. I think you might get where I'm going with this interruption.

When she finally paused long enough for me to interrupt her, I very quickly snuck in a quick question of my own: "Didn't you marry this man and give him two babies?" She of course stopped dead in her tracks, which then placed me about three steps in front of her when I finally stopped. I turned to look at her and she looked up at me and said loudly, "Girl yes, but I was different back then, it wasn't really me. You know, I wasn't even in my right mind!"

So let's take it back some. Perhaps this phrase is familiar to you: "Have you lost your mind?" Or this one: "Have you lost your cotton-picking mind?" Or even this one: "Have you lost your ever-loving mind?" I promise, I can almost hear my mother's voice in my head asking me one of those questions over and over again when I was growing up. To be honest, I often wondered what would make her think that I had somehow lost my mind. You can imagine how, to a young child, this phrase seemed preposterous. Did she really believe my head opened up and my mind somehow fell out? Had I somehow misplaced it, or left it at school yesterday or maybe even left it outside when I was playing? I am, of course, being playful and a

24

tad bit sarcastic, but admittedly it took me a while before I realized that what she really meant was that my behavior was somehow displaying that my mind was not engaged. My behavior was indicating to her that my mind was absent from my body and the outcome of whatever I was doing was going to lead to my behind paying for my mind's absentmindedness!

Almost every action we do starts with our mind and, even when our mind is on autopilot, it is still engaged. It is just engaged in such a way that it is operating based on the familiarity of a rotation that's been put in place so many times that it can operate without the rest of the body paying attention. In order for us to move towards a life-changing transformation that takes us to the end destination that most of us believe with all of our hearts we are supposed to achieve, we have to begin with renewing this incredible, brilliant, awesome tool called the mind!

Romans 12:2 says: "Do not conform to the pattern of this world, but be transformed by the renewing of your mind. Then you will be able to test and approve what God's will is - His good, pleasing and perfect will."

Now, lest you believe that this is an easy, one-time endeavor, please let me inform you that this is a lifelong process that even the best of us struggle with from time to time. Getting the thoughts in our mind to line up with our desired outcomes is a discipline that can take years to develop. Before that sentence sends you into a mini depressive state, let me tell you that you are not alone. Great biblical characters, famous scientists, Ph.D.'s, Grammy winners, Oscar winners, Vice Presidents, everyday moms and dads have all gone to war with the powerful and ever-ready-to-spar mind. The reason we are required to put so much intentional fuel into this mental machine that opposes the forward trajectory that we are trying to move in is that *its* strength is far greater than we have the power or the discipline to overcome. From music that does not uplift to television that tears down, to not reading and stimulating our minds, it is no wonder that when it is time to think, our brains are looking to be entertained once again by a simple plot and lifeless rhetoric that does not need to be chewed before digesting to be understood.

Look at the things that fight for our mind's space: there is social media from Instagram to Twitter, Snapchat to Facebook. From the time we wake up in the morning most of us are reaching for our smart phones to see what has been posted while we were sleeping. The preoccupation with who liked our last post, or better yet didn't like our last post, has almost become a job in and of itself. Our mental state can be determined before 7 o'clock in the morning based on how many likes or comments we've garnered or by what we've seen on the pages of those we believe we're in competition with. If page stalking paid money, many of us would be wealthy based on the sheer value of time we have spent looking at other people's pages and contemplating the relevancy of their life and the authenticity of their posts. We don't realize how much mental space and energy we are wasting by not being present in our own world.

Beyond social media there is the drama that comes from relationships that long should have been put to bed. Boundaries have been crossed and negativity is a constant and familiar partner. It is these relationships that you have told yourself time and time again must go that steal your joy, your peace of mind and your ease of movement (grace). Once these are gone, the ability to be creative and the ability to have vision for tomorrow begins to dissipate. Once drama gets started in the mind, the all-consuming, infamous "he said, she said" commentary or "what I should have said" regret commentary begins to take up the space that was once set aside for new and fresh ideas. It takes up space that was designated to hear up and coming new people who have a story that is invigorating, inspiring and exciting.

The battle for our minds can be won, but it requires putting in work and feeding our minds with that which can fuel our creativity, stimulate our emotions and move us to action. When was the last time you made a reading plan to read 5 -10 books in a year or to listen to the top 10 best sellers on audio book? What new thing have you learned lately? How many new people have you met or have you decided it is your old four and no more? Are you guarding your mind from corrosive television and internet activity or are you consuming anything and everything that comes your way just so you can say you are in the know? Have you allowed gossip to replace real news? Are you the watering hole for people to get the latest information on everybody's life while yours is becoming the cesspool of corrosion? You have one mind and you have one life. When I was growing up there was a commercial that would show some pretty devastating events and then they would show their tagline which was simply "a mind is a terrible thing to waste." Can I tell you... it still is!

I want to challenge you to protect it, guard it, feed it, RENEW IT! Start today by protecting what goes in; the old adage "garbage in, garbage out" is still true. Daily spend time meditating in silence. Allow God to speak to you in the stillness of your heart and mind. The Word of God says, "But we have the mind of Christ" (1 Corinthians 2:16b). There you have the secret weapon. You are halfway to transformation when you consider the fact that you have the mind of Christ to help you. There is no exact or right way; you just need to make it happen. I ask many of my clients to take the first 10-15 minutes of the morning to sit in silence, clear their mind and ask God to give them the plan for the day. Sit and just breathe in and out and let all your cares go to the One who can handle them. Then give God your issues and the things you cannot handle. Worship Him for being the amazing God that He is and let that go where it goes and then sit so He can speak to your heart. Finally, read if you want or get to your day, but be mindful that He is still on the line to speak and listen. You can do this. I know you can. 2 Timothy 1:7 says, "For God hath not given us the spirit of fear; but of power, and of love, and of a sound mind." So come on, get to it. Start with a mindset reset and the rest will be so much easier. For as a person thinks in their heart, so they are (Proverbs 23:7). Question, what are you thinking?

This is Going to Take Heart!

Heart! We all have one, can't live without one. True, lasting transformation takes a strong, healthy heart. Most of us wish we could magically wake up one morning to find that all the adjustments needed for change have been made for us. We want good attributes such as discipline and integrity to suddenly be a part of our nature, and bad habits like being trifling or lazy to magically shift out of our character. Unfortunately, that only occurs in the movies - really bad fantasy movies. In real life we have a responsibility to work it out, to daily walk it out step by step, and to go through a *process* of transformation. Yes, my friend, it takes commitment and personal conviction, a full-on mind and heart shift!

Going through a process of change in any area of life is not for the faint of heart. There will be days when your heart will want to give way to your emotions and quitting will be at the top of your to-do list. I have had days where I have wanted to quit every hour on the hour and every other minute in between. If any of you are like me, and I am guessing you are, there have been days when you have felt like your heart could not take another defeat, another crazy email or phone call with bad news and please don't let anyone else ask me to do something! Those are the days when you have to find the perseverance to dig deep and feel the beat of your own heart and know that you were created for a more abundant life than the one you currently live. Know that it's in you, not just from a possessions perspective but from a soul-ish, emotional, intellectual and social perspective.

In the normal course of life, the heart functions to pump blood through the body, provide oxygen and nutrients to the tissues and remove carbon dioxide and waste. Simply put, the heart naturally facilitates blood which adds life and gets rid of waste. Emotionally, it would appear that the heart has similar functions if we let it do its job. Sometimes we need fresh, uncontaminated air for our emotions to recalibrate and balance out. That also means that there are times and seasons where we need to get rid of some things that are harmful to us if we are going to see the change we desire, the change that is required for a powerful life.

Because you are reading this I already know that your heart beats for more. I encourage you to take heart in believing that you have what it takes to begin a process of transformation that will catapult you into the next phase of your life. You have the heart to stay the course. You have the heart to persevere. You have the heart to become who you were created to be! There is more in you even if it feels like you are at the end of your rope and there are not many beats left in you.

I was recently talking to a friend who is going through a divorce that she never saw coming. She said to me that she felt like her heart was being torn apart into a million pieces. What was once a vibrant, alive and exciting relationship with the man of her dreams had turned into a nightmare of a relationship with arguing, fussing and fighting reminiscent of World War II. Her three children were the causalities being tormented in the middle of the fray. She wondered how a heart that seemed to be filled with nothing but love could be filled now with hatred and distrust.

She was perplexed at the capacity of the heart to hold two such powerful but opposite emotions so deeply and be able to switch between them in an instant. She recalled her wedding day and how she did not think she could feel anything other than incredible, overwhelming love for this man who she was convinced that she was going to spend the rest of her life with. Now, she admitted, being in the same room or even having a conversation with him took every bit of civility and decorum she could muster and that was only for the sake of her kids. I listened intently with sadness and compassion as my friend filled me in and caught me up on the events of her life, but that comment about the depth of the heart and its capacity stuck with me and I have pondered it over the past few weeks. If the heart can shift between love and hate, two powerful sentiments, if it can hold such formidable and weighty emotions, then surely it is one the strongest muscles we have in our body.

So let's think about your heart and its capacity. How many times have you been surprised at your ability to bounce back? How many times have you been able to love again when you thought you were done, done and done? Have you seen yourself go farther than you thought you could go and marveled at your own self when you realized you had more heart than you thought you had? Think about a situation in life where you needed to stick to something and it took everything in you to do so but you did. What made those situations happen? A personal conviction that emanated from your heart that you were going to hang in there until whatever needed to be completed was done. You have a heart that is capable and more than able to handle a transformation process that moves you closer towards your destiny.

Like any muscle in our body, we have to make sure we don't strain, tear or pull our muscles, ultimately making them inoperable. What this means is that protecting our heart is important and we need to make sure we keep it out of harm's way as much as possible. Proverbs 4:23 says it this way: "Above all else, guard your heart, for everything you do flows from it."

What that means is that healthy people, invigorating environments, fresh atmospheres and regularly exercising your creativity make a wonderful recipe for keeping your heart safe and alive with possibility. Then you can face whatever transitions you need to tackle along your journey. Keeping your heart safe is an intentional act. If left to life's circumstances, our hearts can take a beating from people who are selfish and careless and from our own lackadaisical actions, leaving us broken and hurting. We have to make it our aim to keep our heart (the seat of our soul and emotions) as untangled with foolishness as possible so that the rest of us operate at optimal levels. You and I both know that when your heart is broken or hurting you make bad decisions and your potential is limited.

Today would be a great day to start with looking into the chambers of your heart and doing a checkup. Do you hear a steady, regular heartbeat? Does your heart beat strong and are you energized or are you tired and faint? Whatever your state, it is time to get your heart ready to assist you in your process of transformation. We can't do it without our heart's cooperation and help. Let's begin today with a personal conviction to see our way through the whole process to completion. You have the heart to do this, you have the heart to make the changes you want, you have the heart to be a better you, and you have the heart to start today!

Lions Aren't the Only Ones Who Need Courage

Courage - now here is a word that needs revisiting in our culture today. In generations of old, courage was respected and applauded and it meant to be daring, to be different and to take a risk. Those are cute words. In Oakland where I am from, it meant to have guts, hutzpah, to not be a wuss! When old folks talked about having the courage to change for better, the change was not a selfish change. It was for the betterment of oneself so that the family could be better, the community could be better and so society as a whole could be better.

Having the courage to take risks and be transformed, well, to be honest, there is nothing comfortable about this process.

Being courageous to do what others are not willing to do means we may encounter backlash and criticism, but I submit to you that there is something worse and that is to remain stagnant, knowing you need to change and lacking the courage to do so for any reason, but especially the opinions of others. I believe it would be a travesty to live below the standard of what you were created to be simply out of a lack of willingness to move beyond the unknown.

There was a season in my life where I had to take a leap into the unknown and it was truly a difficult decision to make. I worked in corporate America for one of the top entertainment companies in the world (if not the top one): The Walt Disney Company. I was making good money, I was respected, I enjoyed my job and it provided a challenge, something that kept my creativity and mind going to avoid boredom.

There came a point in time, though, where I felt I needed more time to give to what I was purposed to do, not just what I had talent to do. There is a difference. Oftentimes, we start doing a job or any task and, out of dedication to excellence and/or because we are gifted in that area, we end up staying in a permanent place that was originally designed to be temporary. How many friends do you have that got a part-time job in college and the money was better than they had ever had and before long they were doing that job as a full-time career? It was not what they wanted to do or intended to do; they just made decent money at it and stayed too long. The money became the driver, not the passion for the task or job.

In my case, I had the degree and the aptitude to work in finance and to manage money, but I am called to lead people, I am called to inspire, encourage and help people transform their lives and live out their purpose. I could no longer do both effectively. Something had to give. My purpose was calling me to take the risk and leave my easy but fun and challenging, "money in my bank account every Thursday morning like clockwork for the previous 25-years" job, and to step out in faith and trust that by operating in my purpose the money would follow.

Now I want to be clear, I am not talking about quitting my job without a plan on a whim. No, I mean a well thought out, fighting-against-it-for-a-long-time process that had me delaying the inevitable due to fear of not having the financial stability that I was accustomed to. For a while, I could not see the freedom in operating in my pre-ordained purpose because of my need for security. Truthfully, any job at any given time can come along and lay you off due to the economy or a younger, smarter, faster-working employee, so the security we feel is often not real security in the first place.

The day came when after going part-time as a "compromise" (that did not work), I realized that the only way was to take the leap and muster up the courage to write the letter of resignation and turn it in. I had written several, though I had never actually submitted them to HR or my boss who was supportive of my career shift. Without looking back... well maybe I looked back a few times when my savings was going down and not up... I jumped. I walked away from my job and into my purpose, and although it meant cutting our household income in half, somehow 8 years later we have been and are doing just fine. The doors that have opened up and the opportunities I have been able to take advantage of around the world have been rich and rewarding because I had the courage to make the move. Have there been days when I have missed working in that environment? Absolutely there have. But there are no regrets in operating in my purpose.

I have been changed in the process. By choosing to courageously go after what I was designed to do, I exposed myself to the opportunity to be transformed by encounters with people I otherwise would not have met. I have been impacted by experiences that have transformed my thinking and broadened my view. New thoughts and waves of creativity have bombarded me and moved me into position to impact others in a more profound way. These came about because of having courage to do what some thought was an outlandish idea: leave my comfort zone of the unknown and leap into the possibility of faith and see what could be in my life. Can you take the leap of courage today and do what you have been promising yourself to do for forever?

"For God gave us a spirit not of timidity (cowardliness) but of power and love and self-discipline" (2 Tim 2:7).

You have what it takes to go after whatever you have been purposed to do. It may not be easy but you can do it. Here is a promise: the pain and discomfort will be worth it, you and those around you will happier, because you will be operating at your optimal best, you will be operating in your purpose. It is time to allow the transformation process to move forward so that you can see what has been waiting for you and who has been waiting for you to impact their lives for good. Go get 'em, your best days are ahead of you. You have the power, you are loved, God will grace you with the discipline to take the leap of faith and you will see results.

Time to Stop Making Excuses

All of us know at least one person who makes excuses, right? This is a common trait that dates back all the way to the Garden of Eden! You know the story, it's the one where God says to Adam and Eve, "Don't eat the fruit from a particular tree in the garden." Adam and Eve hear him clearly but somehow the serpent (evil) gets to talking to Eve about why she should not eat fruit from that very tree. Now, she should have known something was wrong when she found herself in a conversation with a snake, but that is another story for another day. This serpent engages her in a theological discussion on the thoughts, motives and intentions of God and convinces her to eat the fruit in direct disobedience to God's command.

Eve not only takes a bite, but in an interesting twist in the story so does her husband, Adam, who is standing there right beside her. (Side note - ladies, we have some serious persuasion skills when it comes to the men in our lives. We can get them to do a lot of things - let's always make sure we use that gift for good.) When God finds out they have disobeyed Him, He asks them about it straight up. He then asks them an accountability question and He gets an interesting response from all parties. Adam says, "Well God, it really is *your* fault because you gave me the woman and she made me eat of the fruit." Now we all know we can't make anybody do any-thing, right?! I have always wondered how God took the "it is really your fault" thing. Funny how, when backed into a corner, many of us will still blame God for the is-sues in our lives.

The woman says, "It was the serpent's fault, he gave me the apple and he tricked me by saying you were hiding stuff from us and I would be smart if I ate it." Notice she did not own the fact that she believed a lie from the ultimate liar himself. Remember, they had everything they needed in the garden so there was no reason to think that God was keeping anything from them. What could have possibly been missing in their lives? If there was something, they would never have known it, for things were truly perfect in their lives. The serpent looked around and realized that he had no one to blame, but my guess is if there had been someone else there he would have blamed it on them, as no one was owning their own behavior.

Today, people are still making excuses for their behavior just like they did in Genesis 3. It is always somebody else's fault and ownership of our own stuff has long gone out the window. How do you respond to failures, mishaps or downright wrong choices? How are you at owning your own behavior and being responsible for your own actions? Many of us spend most of our time telling the story we want others to believe which has someone else starring in the key role of "why I am not doing..." or "keeping me from..." this and that. The ability to live in a place of truth regarding why we are where we are is a function of being honest with ourselves first. We have to be truthful enough with ourselves to admit when we lack the discipline to dot all the Is and cross all the Ts.

We have to get rid of the fake reasons for our laziness, if that is truly what it is. I had a friend where many of us could almost take out a list and guess what excuse she was going to give for why her life was a mess. You know some of them and have heard others use them: I just don't have enough time, I don't have the same connections everybody else has, I am less talented than those who are doing what I want to do, I don't have enough money or resources, it is too late to start now, I did not have the right family or the right atmosphere to help me, I don't have the support, I don't learn as fast... and the list goes on and on. Now I know most of you don't use any of these to justify why you are not pursuing your purpose, but believe me other people do.

I was listening to a kid the other day explain why he did not get his work done and he said that he had nothing to say because he had used up all the excuses he could think of in his head. I had so much respect for that kid in that moment because I know some adults who could never be that honest. They just recycle the same excuses over and over again hoping they can fool the listener or that the listener doesn't remember they have used that excuse 50 times before.

Now let's be clear, I am not talking about real setbacks and things that are not in your control. That is called life: things happen and we have to adjust when they do. However, we can't even let those things be a reason we don't pursue our purpose by looking to overcome the obstacle. Many others have encountered setbacks and legitimate obstacles to progress, but when you really want it, you look to work around it and press past those things as opposed to letting them be the determining factor as to whether you get to the place you desire. Don't let life's setbacks be a perpetual distraction for you. Let them come and go and get on with your goals and work with everything you have in you. The more time you spend making excuses, the more likely you are to begin to believe them. This will become your calling card, leaving you with virtually no confidence or hope.

So how do we stop making excuses? First, own your own behavior and be truthful with yourself. In looking to move to the next phase of our lives, it is imperative that we own our behaviors (good and bad) and not blame others for that which squarely sits on our own shoulders. You can't fix what you won't acknowledge is broken!

Second, we have to make a decision that we are not going to let legitimate life circumstances be the bomb that blows up our entire plan. Look for alternatives and work arounds to the perceived setback and keep moving forward. Know that things will come up. That is how it goes in life. In fact, there is a scripture that says you will have trouble in this life; that is just how it is (John 16:33 paraphrased). No one escapes this truth. Another helpful step is to write down the opposite of what your excuse is in a journal, your phone, a notepad, iPad or scratch paper. This takes work and discipline but is extremely helpful. When you hear yourself making an excuse for why you can't do something, write it down and write down the reasons that this is not true or not the whole story. Remind yourself that this is an excuse and there is a way around it.

Finally, take note of the fact that you are more than capable of fulfilling your destiny and purpose but it takes work and it will not come easy - nothing worth anything usually does. There will be challenges, there will be days you feel like quitting, there will be days when you want to blame the system, other nationalities, your family, your shape, your color, your hair and the dog, but remember you were made for greatness and there is no room for excuses or blame. Trust me, just keep going or, in the words of Dory from the movie Nemo, "just keep swimming." You will be glad you did in the end!

The Death of Mediocrity

"Most likely to be Mediocre!" Have you ever noticed no school yearbook has this category? No one is vying for votes to win this award or title in their last year of high school or college. There are no awards shows, no mediocre academies, no trophies and no medals given out to those who show a high degree of average proficiency. If any of you are like me, you have many incredibly productive seasons where you are flying high, kicking behind and taking names. Seemingly invincible, everything is operating in high gear and nothing seems to be able to stop you until that one thing falls apart and somehow, some way your train pulls in the station and overnight your high octane engine stalls. Restarting seems difficult and what ensues is a slow-motion, weighted-down version of yourself that frustrates you and moves your needle to the dreaded red zone called mediocrity.

To be mediocre is to allow the quality of what we do to drop to a level that is not reflective of the high standard we are capable of, or at least lower than what we have traditionally put out. It is substandard, low level, just enough, so-so, just getting by, you know the "it'll do" mentality. It is not our best and for sure it is not what we are proud of! I can hear a mentor of mine, Pastor Bam Crawford, quoting St. Jerome all the time saying, "Good, better, best. Never let it rest. Till your good is better and your better is best." This always rings loudly in my ears when I find myself slipping into a funk, when I realize I am trapped in that nerve-racking conflict between what should be versus what reality is. Mediocrity has a way of bringing with it a certain feeling of guilt and shame because deep down inside we know we are made for more and have better in us.

The power questions become: What should be done in order to get the desired changes we want? How do we pull out of the station of "good enough" when we know there is more, there is better in us? How do we do this especially when those around us may be prone to accept the lesser version of our offerings because it is better than what they could accomplish? The answer is you have to die to your **acceptance of mediocrity for yourself,** even if those around you would gladly accept it as okay. You have to decide that ideas like *average* and *good enough* are enemies of your progress towards greatness.

You have not been created to be average. You have known all your life that

there is more in you and that you were designed to do something significant. You
cannot settle for mediocre, less than or just
enough. It won't satisfy and it isn't you. So
you have to raise the bar, raise your sights
and raise your expectations of yourself and
see beyond today to greatness. It will cost
you your mediocre thinking. The price may
be high but the reward is greater.

How do you know you were created
for more than the average person? Well,
let's explore this thought a little deeper for
a bit. First of all, you are reading this book.
People who are not interested in changing
and being their best would not pick up a
book on change or transformation. I am
guessing that you are hungry to be the best
you that you can be and you know that you
have not arrived yet, even if you have experienced some measure of success. Reading, studying and trying to get to the core

of your issues to address the low hanging fruit is important to you. There has always been a feeling in you that you could do more and be more. Either from childhood or as far back as you can remember there has seemingly been a call or something that sits on your life and designates you as different from others. Not better, not superior, just a little different. You don't broadcast it, you don't tell it to everybody, but secretly inside you there is something that you know you have been specifically called to do and you can't get away from it. You may not yet know what that thing is, you just know that something is there and it compels you to set yourself apart to some degree so that you are ready for it.

In my life I have always been picked to lead. As far back as I can remember every time I have been in any situation

where a leader was needed, I have somehow always been chosen. If I go to jury
duty, after hearing a case when we retreat
to the jury room before any words can be
exchanged, before I open my mouth,
someone will look at me and say "You look
like a leader, I pick you." They vote and I
end up being the foreman. If I am in a
classroom and groups are picked, I am
chosen as the group leader. That has happened to me all my life and I have not been
able to get away from it. Eventually I realized that I have been called to lead and I
quit fighting it. You, too, have had signs
along the way that you have been called to
greatness. You go along with the level of
everyone else but there is that nagging
feeling in you that continues to annoy you.
There is a voice in there calling you to
tweak it, improve it, and work it until it is
the best you can make it. You have heard

it. It has been in you for a long time, hiding behind the shadow of mediocrity.

Now that you have figured out what the obstacle is that keeps you from operating at the level and getting the results you want, it is time to tell mediocrity goodbye. It takes guts and it has to be intentional. It is far too easy in our microwave generation to take for granted the ease and pleasures of life and to forget that you get out of something what you put into it. Galatians says it this way, "Don't be deceived, God is not mocked, whatever you sow, and that is what you reap." Did you catch that? Don't be deceived, tricked, bamboozled, and hoodwinked. Whatever you plant, you will reap that harvest. It is a principal even if it does not look like it is true in the moment. Don't buy the lie that you can sow average and reap greatness. When we welcome mediocrity and allow it to take up residence inside us, we have to know it has no boundaries. It is not confined to a particular area. You may intend to just be average in one thing but you don't always get to choose where the mediocrity will show up. It is like going on a diet: you can hope weight will be lost all over but for me it goes from my face first and then the rest of my body. This is like mediocrity - it creeps into all areas of our lives and then takes over.

Today is the day you can declare and decree that you are created for greatness and you will get there. You are going to pursue each day with purposeful attention to the details of living the best you can be, not comparing yourself to others but being the best you. That means giving your best to what you do professionally, studying your craft whatever that may be. Taking a class, studying a new way of business, learning a new trick of the trade, updating a skill set, improving your résumé with something, working on your image, social media presence - whatever will move you just that much closer to the best you that you can be. Remember good, better, best, here a little, there a little. It does not all have to be done in a day. Incremental changes that move the needle towards greatness are all that is required. Surprise yourself today as you move towards a better you and leave mediocrity behind. Greatness is a much better companion and has better benefits and a memorable ending!

The Whole Truth

Remember the old court shows or movie scenes where someone went on the stand and they were asked to put their hand on a Bible and swear to tell the truth, the whole truth? They ended with "So help me God!" Perhaps you have noticed that truth today no longer seems to be absolute. Truth is tantamount to whatever I want it to be and whatever suits my current situation. In fact, it changes when I need it to so that it fits my reality. It seems everybody has a version of it and it seems to change and bend whenever it is convenient. Most of us have a bio, a resume; a story that we tell that puts us in our best light before others. It does not matter to us that we have embellished some parts of the narrative. We have omitted things that would not make us look good and we have edited it so that when the story is heard or read we come out looking on top.

This is commonplace today because most of us are not interested in the truth because truth makes us pay attention to it, it demands recognition. Truth will not be bent into what we need it to be to feed our ego or stroke our narcissistic tendencies. No truth holds its place anchored by honesty and reality, and dares us to look it in the eye and stay the same. Those who love truth change to fit what the truth is, not the other way around. Truth holds its narrative and does not shift based on the circumstances.

In order to have real transformation in our lives we have to live in a place of truth and respect its demands. We cannot weave made-up facts into our reality and expect to land in a place of authenticity and honor. In fact, the more we uncover our
74

true selves and the true story we are living, the more we are able to relate to one another and speak life to one another. Not long ago I had to look at some hard, cold truths about myself and why I was in the rut I was in. For some time I had assumed that my circumstances, which were harsh and uninspiring the previous five years, had wreaked havoc on my mind, emotions and spirit. I was tired of everything and everybody. I was tired of my marriage, pastoring, counseling, casting vision, and managing money. Just tired!

I went on a field trip to D.C. with my 10-year-old daughter and her school and one day I stayed back at the hotel to write. I began to reflect on my life. I had spun a story in my head and heart which was now on auto-play about *why* I felt the emptiness that I had been feeling for quite some time.

It was the prior years of life and its challenges, it was the amount of time I spent alone, it was the fact that I started everything late in life (having babies, becoming a pastor, etc.). It was not growing up with a godly legacy or pastor parents, my husband and I having to grind out ministry on our own as an independent church. All of this was factually true and played like a movie trailer in my mind whenever I felt down and uninspired or hopeless. On days when it was really out of control, I envied friends in ministry who had come from a legacy of pastors or parents in ministry who had taken them to church since they were 2 days old or had been mentored by pastors and groomed for ministry.

I longed for mentors who had been in business and could teach me more than I had already learned from MBA School and trial and error on my own. I wished for some female who was experienced in my role to pull me to the side and say "I've got you, stick with me and I will help you get to your ultimate purpose." I wanted a manager, coach, or a mentor. I wanted someone who could take this journey with me and help. The truth is, God had been calling me into a deeper place with Him for years and I was looking for someone physical and fleshly. I knew in the back of my head the spiritual Calvary was not coming, but I still looked for it. I even put some of my life on hold waiting for it, all the while knowing that my journey was going to be one in which the lessons came from sitting at His feet.

While in D.C. that weekend I read something that made me look at truth in a new way. I can't tell you what it was but somewhere in my mind and heart I realized

that the common denominator in my griev-
ances was me. I had told the same tired
story to myself so many times it had become my truth. I did not realize I was creating a self-fulfilling prophecy concerning
myself. I was speaking aloneness and iso-
lation into being. Now before you get
weirded out and think I am headed down
the path of you will name it and claim it and
it will be, I mean talking yourself into defeat where your actions start to line up with
whatever you are telling yourself and believing. I was speaking death to my own
dreams and creating a truth of negativity
by accepting what the circumstances were
instead of what God said about me.

His truth was what I needed to speak
over my life, not what my circumstances
dictated to me. That weekend I knew I had
to change or transformation would never
happen in my own life and I desperately

needed it; my future depended upon it.

Truth has to be a standard for our lives and we have to know that it is set in concrete and anchored in place so that we can measure progress and have a baseline to build our lives upon. Loving the truth can be your best friend and can catapult you into a dimension of wholeness that can be extremely rewarding. I can hear you asking: how might that be? Simply put, loving the truth takes deception out of living.

Being honest with yourself and with those in your sphere of influence gives you the grace to be at peace with conversations, puts you in a position to not have to worry about what you said or to have to remember or live a lie. In your assessment of yourself, truth cuts down on how long it takes to get to the core of your issues, which means you can get to solutions faster. Transparency becomes real when truth is used as the magnifying glass. Finally, in the age of "staged reality TV" it is refreshing when we have the ability to live in the light of truth and be transformed into something people can see, feel and touch and know that it is real and authentic.

That weekend I wrote down the negative script that I had played as a movie in my mind and then rewrote the script with a positive spin. Just having a new reference point, a new plot, a new positive theme to my mindset helped take the negativity out of my head. I read and rewrote the script over and over again until it made better sense based on who I know I am called to be, not who the past said I was or who people may believe I am. I still refer to it from time to time, as it takes time to reprogram your mindset, but it is possible with truth! I used scripture, quotes and truth to rewrite the lying script and began to rehearse the truth. As a Christian, I have to admit my rewrite was scripture-laden because that is the foundation of truth for me. It had things like Romans 8:28: "All things work together for those that love Him and are called according to His purpose." Philippians 4:13: "I can do all things through Christ who strengthens me." Psalm 139:14: "I will praise You, for I am fearfully *and* wonderfully made; marvelous are Your works, and *that* my soul knows very well." And my favorite: "'For I know the plans I have for you,' declares the Lord, 'plans to prosper you and not to harm you, plans to give you hope and a future'" (Jeremiah 29:11). These and others, along with truth commentary about what is real, began to reshape the story in my head. This is not the only way to reshape the landscape in your mind, but might just help get you on the road to the whole truth!

Who Are You Talking to Like That?

I have a very gifted friend who for years has wanted to get into the voiceover industry. She has a number of characters that she has created and given voice to that range in ethnicity and age. She gives them personality and sass that she uses to audition her skills. Many of us also have a similar audition tape that runs in our heads as well, only that tape plays to an audience of one (ourselves), and it plays on repeat with tones and words that are not healthy or conducive to our success.

It is that voice in your head that reminds you of what you can and cannot do, who you are not, what you don't have, who you are not like, what you have missed out on and what you won't accomplish. In movies or cartoons, voiceovers are an external voice that is often laid over a scene to tell what is happening and give voice to pictures or a character. This allows the viewer access to the story that the creator wants them to believe is happening.

For us, our narrative often arises out of our past experiences, our parents, authority figures in our lives or relationships that are causing anxiety. Consequently, these circumstances lend themselves to the voices in our heads not being the most positive of voices. Like an old-school tape recorder, our psyche has the incredible ability to remember things said to us, scientists tell us, as early as the womb. So if unwanted in the womb, if perceived as a burden as a child, if told our look was too much like our "no good daddy," these cruel commentaries can auto replay with a wicked twist. Our voice is later switched out for the original voice and we hear our own voice repeating these cruelties with regularity, stunting our growth and rendering us paralyzed from forward progress. These voices must be reevaluated and replaced in their content!

Truthfully, the mind is a brilliant tool; it has the ability to function on autopilot after minimal cycles. Once you have allowed your mind to get into a negative conversation cycle it will literally take over and run that conversation all by itself without your help and repeat it daily, hourly, even every five minutes without you even being aware of its groove. In order for the transformation that we are talking about to really occur in the fullest and richest way possible, it is necessary that we change our self-talk to that which speaks to the change and the end result that we desire. The cycle has to be broken so that you are free from the negativity and released to be creative and productive. Your creativity cannot thrive in a negative incubator.

I encourage my clients to reevaluate and replace the content of their internal conversation, as opposed to engaging that voice. We talk to ourselves - that is a reality. My grandmother used to say there is nothing wrong with talking to yourself. It is when you start answering yourself that you have to start worrying! Reevaluating the content is a wonderful process because you can take that same voice and redirect it to positive energy by changing the script. This is far easier than stopping the voice altogether.

Sometimes I will have clients write a new script filled with the verbiage that speaks to who they want to become and to traits that they want to be a part of their character. Then they repeat it until it is memorized so that their mind has something new to focus on. I have also done this in times past while evaluating what I say to myself. It helps me have the opportunity to see what kinds of things are lingering in my soul and bringing me down. This is not the only way to change your self-talk, but one I have found helpful personally and with my clients.

I had a client who once said that when she would wake up in the morning she would begin to hear an audio track in her head like a Bose surround sound system filled with demeaning and degrading things about her body, her intelligence, her decision making ability and things similar to this. She said once the loop would start, it would continue as if she had her own stereo system in her brain. After we spent some time together and I got a chance to know her and her life, I found out that she was dating a guy who, when upset, would spew all kinds of horrible and degrading things at her. She had a pattern of dating men who belittled her and tore her self-esteem down, repeating a scene she had played out countless times with her father. Now, neither her father nor the men she dated had to say anything. Her own self-talk did the negative talking for them starting at the top of the morning. Reevaluating one's self talk and the content of it can help us deal with some relationship issues and perhaps allow us to let some people and situations go that are causing us to have to those perpetual conversations in our head that leave us devastated and hurt.

However, you get there, whether you rewrite the script you speak or you get rid of that which is causing you to have a negative conversation, you have to be intentional about changing the conversation. Whatever you do, get the negativity out of your head so that you are not sabotaging your own destiny. Make a new voiceover for the story of your life and tell the story you want the world to know. Rewrite the script and recalibrate your mind. Let it reflect the truth that you are powerful, you are beautiful, you are full of life and you have a future that is bright and filled with possibility. Can you hear it? I can and it sounds beautiful. It sounds like you!

Pruned to Produce More

Have you ever had to make a tough decision? I mean where the responsibility and the many potential outcomes, both good and bad, sit squarely on your shoulders? If you have, then you know the angst that it causes, the contemplation that can go on day after day, the scenarios we play out in our head wondering if we have settled on the right decision. Tough decisions are just that… tough. Let's face it, they are rough on the mind, our emotions and sometimes even on our bodies. When it comes time to reassess what and who is in our lives and if they are healthy for us, more often than not we have come to a really tough decision place. Today we need to look at what needs to be discarded from our lives. This power move is one of the toughest we may encounter in our trans-formation journey. It is tough because it requires many of the power moves that are in this book. It requires truth, transpar-ency, confidence, heart, discipline and self-care and an unmitigated resolve and cour-age to get out of our comfort zone.

There are times and seasons where some things simply need to come to an end. Flowers need to be pruned in order to grow; the split ends of our hair need to be cut in order for our hair to be healthy. It is a part of life, but it is a very difficult part of life. Too often we allow ourselves to be-come comfortable with dysfunction and the thought of letting go of knowing how we will feel without whatever *it* is can be a scary thing for many of us. The fear can be so great it can cause us to put off doing what we know is necessary and dealing with a less-than-healthy relationship

simply because we are afraid of the unknown. Sometimes we are not convinced
that getting rid of dead weight or toxic circumstances will actually make our loads
lighter. After all, we have become accustomed to carrying this weight now. Many of
us have grown so comfortable with the ex-
tra weight that we carry it around like a security blanket and we wrap it around us to
protect us from we don't even know what.

Both my daughters have a lot of hair.
Here is where I wonder what God was
thinking in giving me girls, as I am not
great with doing hair at all! One has full,
do-anything-with-it hair. Press it and it is
long, wet it and it curls up nice. When she
gets older she will appreciate the ability to
have many options. The other has long
wavy hair that pulled from my Indian
mother and grandfather. Hers is whisper
fine when heat is applied and long spiral

curls when wet. The latter is not as versatile but has its own undeniable properties that make people say she has good hair! Recently both of them went to the shop to get their hair done and our family stylist said that they needed their ends cut, as they both had split ends. With split ends, the hairs' outer protective layer is stripped away (often times due to hard water and or heat) and the hair underneath is exposed to the elements and splits. Unfortunately, you can't just put a new protective layer on or just put some product on it; you have to cut the dead ends off and allow the hair relief.

When she heard she needed her hair cut, one of my daughters was not only offended at the thought, but vehemently responded that she was not allowing her hair to be cut, not just that day, but ever! It took some really age appropriate convincing that she would be better as a result of cutting off the bad and allowing the good to not only grow but shine! The stylist did something helpful: she had her feel their hair before she cut it. Afterwards, when they ran their hands through it and they felt how silky soft it was and how radiant it looked, they understood why they had to cut the dead part off. Both of them have experienced hair growth since and I must admit this has sort of backfired a little. My oldest has decided that if cutting an inch off resulted in such great results, she should get it cut every time she goes... that is a whole other conversation!

There is a time and season to everything (Ecclesiastes 3:1); we have to prune our lives so that we can heal, grow, and live lighter without the dead relationships and events that weigh us down. There is another aspect to pruning that plays in. When things leave our lives beyond our control, we grieve the loss. But there is some measure of relief that we had it happen *to us* and we were merely responding. The more difficult issue is when we need to make the adjustment and prune back ourselves - that is an entirely different situation. There are times in our lives when we need to do some pruning and cut back on some activities. There are other times when some people are no longer healthy for us and are toxic to our forward progress. They are helping to lead us to a dead end, wasting time and emotions. Pruning our lives does not have to be a rude or nasty process. It is just a tough but necessary ending that can yield untold benefits. In some instances, you may still have love but are simply no longer able to have them in your inner circle. It is possible to love from a distance.

So go ahead, assess your village and see if you need to do some pruning. Growth happens after you cut the bad parts away. It does not mean the people are bad; they just may be bad for you in this season of life. You may be able to reconnect in another season after growth has occurred, perspectives have changed or maturity sets in, but either way you are going to be alright.

You may be okay in your relationships; your circle may be healthy, encouraging, truthful and adding to your purpose. If so, you are blessed that this is not your issue and this power move is one that you can put on the shelf for another day. However, if adjustments need to be made, give yourself that gift and have the courage to do what is in the best interest of the transformation of life that you are after. I promise you won't regret the care you give yourself and the growth and shine will be apparent to all who benefit from your purposed life.

Paralyzed by

Procrastination

So it took me forever to write this particular power move. Is that any surprise to you given the title of the chapter? Shocker! Yes, I too can be a procrastinator. Many of us, even the most successful of us, if we are not plagued with perpetual distractions, are procrastinators. We wait until the last minute to do what could have been done last month or last week. If you are like me then somehow along your journey you were convinced that you have more creativity when the pressure is on, when the clock is ticking down and the adrenaline is pumping. It is true that there can be something said for the adrenaline that flows under pressure and it feels like being on the edge hones our focus to a laser harp intensity. However, if we were to be truly honest, some of us live on the edge of simply not taking care of business until the last minute and it is not adrenaline; it is laziness and poor planning.

The deceptive factor is that we have had some measure of success doing things at the last minute and it has fooled us into believing we are good and cool under pressure, so our last minute antics have become habit. When it does not work out or something unexpected happens, we are left with letting someone down, or having to impose on others, or worse yet doing something in a sub-standard manner because we procrastinated. This feeling of knowing you did not give it your best nags at you and causes unnecessary anxiety, guilt and usually a promise that we are going to start earlier next time, only to fall back into the same pattern again. We are addicted to procrastination.

I started my last minute shenanigans in college. Everything else seemed far more important and interesting than that paper that was due or whatever the assignment was. I managed to at least get a B and sometimes could pull out an A and so I began to believe I operated better this way. I convinced myself I was better waiting until the pressure was high. It carried over into my work life but the stakes here are higher and the repercussions costlier. Even so, I could pull out a financial report, make a presentation or give an update with very little time left on the clock and it kept me thinking that my good memory and my quick-on-my-feet approach was optimal. It wasn't until I started ministering at churches that this caught up with me because, although my physical audience was the crowd gathered on a Sunday morning, my heart knew that the one watching and taking inventory was the one who called me into ministry in the first place and He was not pleased with a last minute effort of preparation. Colossians 3:23 says, "And whatever you do, do it heartily, as to the Lord and not to men."

I remember once talking to my therapist about this 11:59:59 approach to life and she said something really profound: If I was good at the last minute, how great could I be if I took more time on it? It was a revelatory moment for me, for I had never even stopped to think that I could be exponentially better if I started sooner and took my time to let it marinate in my heart, mind and spirit. I thought of it like a good pot of seafood gumbo. It is good the first day it is cooked, but if allowed to settle overnight, the next day the flavors have blended together and marinated in such a way that the flavor is so much better over time than immediately when prepared. I realized that if I did not put off until tomorrow what I could do today, I would actually have tomorrow for a review, or to have someone critique it for me and work out the kinks, making it that much better.

So what is it that makes us put things off when we don't intend to or when we know we should be working on a particular thing but can't quite seem to get into position? For many of us, it is our desire to do something else that we believe is more exciting. For others, it is our inability to enact self-control over how we feel. Our emotions are not under control and so we are moved by them. We never want to do what is critical, especially if something else that takes less effort and seemingly gives a quicker emotional payoff is readily available. We need to arrest our emotions and enact some discipline to get started and finish that which requires our attention.

There will always be something that is more fun to do with our time, but it is critical to allow ourselves a shot at producing something great that flows out of a peaceful, unstressed mind. Planning and executing a plan will help us transform into productive and efficient deliverers of a body of work that has been born out of intention and purpose, not reckless throwing together of information that gets it done but may lack the finishing touches that only a plan and time can garner.

As we work on becoming better, it would be a wonderful change for those who procrastinate to work into our plan the grace of time to do a task better. As a power move for this module, for the next 7 days try to make a plan around what you need to get done and work on those critical items in advance of them being due. See how you feel, note if there is any improvement in your stress level and the flow of your creativity. This may seem silly or even trivial, but you have to start somewhere. It is always better to make adjustments on your own as opposed to being forced to make changes because life requires you to. Let's make a commitment to stop waiting and procrastinating to begin making the necessary changes in our lives and be our own inspiration for change. Let's get to the benefits that will come along with our new self now! Go ahead and write down the plan for the next week and, if you are bold, make one for the things you want to accomplish or have to accomplish this month. The worst that can happen is that the plan changes!

Change the Atmosphere!

There was a commercial back in the 90s that showed people who were stuck in a rut everyday as they were headed to lunch and the tag line uttered by one co-worker was, "Same place?" and the other co-worker responded with, "Same place." "Same time?" "Same time." "Same thing?" "Same thing!" The routine they were showing was them eating the same food every day. And clearly that day was going to be no different.

I remember working at Northrop Aircraft right out of college. I worked with some really fun women and each day at lunch we all looked at each other and knew we were headed out of those drab blue and gray partitions and to the parking lot to one of our cars. We did not have to say any-thing; we just automatically knew we were headed to Taco Bell. Yep, that is right - good, old Taco Bell. Looking back now, I am not even sure how that started or why, but we went to Taco Bell for lunch every day (it seemed) for at least a year for no apparent reason. We all made really good money and we were relatively smart women with degrees, some of us multiple ones, but we threw down Burrito Supremes and Taco Supremes like it was nothing. I think I still have a layer or two on my be-hind and hips from those days.

Oftentimes, for transformation to oc-cur in our lives, we have to make a change to our atmosphere and our routine. We have to change where we work or how we work. We have to get out of our regular routine or get one. One would be surprised to find how much our surroundings have an impact on our perspective, our moods, our emotional state and our spiritual well-being. Simple things like light, music, color, temperatures and fabrics all affect us positively or negatively. I am not suggesting that we all become super ultra-sensitive and have our moods shifting with the slightest breeze. What I am saying is that we have to look at what kind of energy we are allowing to affect us and where that energy is coming from.

You may not believe this, but there is a spiritual and a natural realm and energy flows in both realms and affects us tremendously. Energy is fluid, powerful and persuasive. When our atmosphere is filled with energy that is positive, all is well. When that energy is negative, our world can be filled with depression and despondency. We are disillusioned, discontent, dissatisfied, disinterested and disengaged! The natural progression is that this leads to stressful situations, conflict, unresolved issues and unsafe atmospheres. In a vicious cycle, this puts undue pressure on our spirits and minds and prevents us from thinking clearly and processing life in a rational and balanced way. Can you see where this cycle is going? I will go down one more layer: if we are not careful, all of this will make us really sensitive to many more things like sad music, dark light, fabrics that are rough on our skin and anything that brings the slightest bit of discomfort to our natural flesh.

More often than not we get stuck and the cycle is unrelenting. All of us pass through these seasons at some point in life, but some of us live in these valleys because we don't know how to get out of these seemingly never-ending highways of craziness. We don't know how to change, how to transform our own lives. Everybody else seems to just be passing us by and we wonder if our day will ever come. I pray that as you read this book some hope is flooding back into your soul because transformation is happening. The small changes add up to big results. This power move of changing your atmosphere is a tough one - I have to admit that. We are addicted to dysfunctional behavior patterns and we go to familiar places on autopilot.

Breaking the cycle takes courage but must be done, even if it's just for minutes a day to get peaceful thoughts. You don't have to do it all at once. Pick one thing to focus on changing and take a few minutes to figure out how that particular transformation move will work in your life. Those few minutes will slowly bring relief so that you can begin to gain some perspective and see what you need to do to change your atmosphere and get to a healthy space.

Today is a new day and you have time to do it. Take a few deep breaths now. If you are a praying person, take a few minutes to pray and slow your mind down and think. What can you change about your routine? What is on autopilot that needs to be rearranged to de-stress your day? What do you do without thinking that, if you paid attention, would not need to be done any-more and would give you more time in your day? Who can you stop catering to? Where can you not go today and it would not make a difference? What could you add that would make you tons more efficient and take a few things off the list? How might adding meditating and prayer in the begin-ning of your day help you to focus and pre-pare yourself for the whole day? Why not start now? It can't hurt, right? Check your life for what needs to be done and do the easiest task if that works for you. For all you know this power transformation move is the one that will get you to your next - a simple adjustment in your atmosphere and there you go, air to breathe... hmmm, who knew breathing would feel so good?!

Next Up... Humility!

Have you ever been around somebody who thinks they have all the answers
or knows every detail about something
they just got wind of yesterday? Doesn't
that drive you crazy? If you are one of
these people, you probably don't know
what in the world I am talking about because you think you really do know it all. I
told you earlier that I recently had the
pleasure of going on my daughter's 5th
grade trip to Washington, D.C. to learn
about our government and how it works. It
was a week-long trip with over 140 people
traveling (it was surprisingly well orga-
nized). In a week's time with that many
kids, you hear some pretty amazing conversations about all kinds of subjects. What

was truly interesting to me was the confidence some of the kids spoke with about things they knew absolutely nothing about. Loudly and with the boldness of a lion, some would share with the other kid's things that were just flat out wrong. The parents listening would sometimes correct the information but often times it was not worth the energy because all of us knew that in short order they would learn the truth and it would be corrected by life experiences. They are kids after all; they don't know what they don't know.

That is okay for kids who are in a long-term season of learning, but what about when we encounter adults who exhibit the same brashness and we all know that they should know better? You know the kind: they have little self-awareness and pride emanates from them in truck loads. They won't ask for directions and would rather stay lost and searching than admit they don't know where they are going. Perhaps you know a few who are so full of their own thoughts that anyone around them has to take a small supporting role because they have the lead all tied up. Most of us grow weary of how taxing these kinds of people are on us and our atmosphere. The real question is: do we have any of these tendencies that are prohibiting our transformation process?

What many of us have not figured out is that is humility is a powerful trait that benefits us and those who interact with us. The ability to ask for help and acknowledge when we are out of our lane is an admirable gift to possess. One thing great leaders learn that makes them even greater leaders is that they don't have to know everything. They just have to have great people around them! Perhaps you are one who is not only trying to transform your life, but your business or your team, as well. Various skill sets may be required to get the job done and, honestly, few of us have been gifted with *all* the gifts. It is pride that keeps us trying to do those things that we may be weak in when we have people around us who have great strength in those areas. What takes us 10 hours to do in an area of low talent could possibly take another one hour if it is their area of strength. So a great question to ask yourself is: why don't I ask for help? Why do I feel the need to handle everything on my own? Sometimes the answer is that we just want to control the process. For others, it is that we don't want to appear weak. Perhaps we don't want to share the credit. I can assure you that whatever it is, it is keeping you from the change you desperately desire.

A little bit of humility goes a long way towards moving us to transformation. C.S. Lewis said, "Humility is not thinking less of yourself, it is thinking of yourself less." Here is where we have to make a conscious effort to stay far away from narcissism and seek to find people who complement us in ways that make us better. We need to intentionally move away from seeing people as competition and instead see the gifts they have that will make our lives more productive and satisfying and make the world around us better.

There is a scripture that says pride comes before the fall and that humility comes before exaltation (Proverbs 16:18). Even Jesus humbled Himself and put on humanity to show us how to walk humbly before God and one another. It is no easy task for some of us, but a necessary one. How do we do it? We take a good, long, deep look inside. We check our motives, we examine how we treat those around us because, truthfully, we reap what we sow. Taking the time to be introspective and look at our heart for arrogance and self-righteousness will help us understand ourselves and what we need to work on. For some of us, we need to ask those around us if they find us prideful or arrogant. That sounds scary but can be a really powerful and useful reflection from someone who loves you and believes in you being the best that you can be. You do this when you find that you are really having trouble seeing yourself and have people around you who will speak truth. You may find that some around you know more than you think they do about your character.

If you are willing, do the hard thing: ask for help assessing your pride level. Ask those who spend the most time with you if they perceive you as a prideful person or if haughtiness is a part of your make-up. See if they see a humble person in you. More than likely, what you learn will make you better and help you transform into the person you want to be. In order to really go through a true transformation process and live on purpose for purpose, humility is a critical element that we can't do without. Let's start today by acknowledging that we have been created for purpose and God's plan is best. Knowing that makes humbling ourselves an easier task because we know that God thought enough of us to create us and give us purpose. Anything else in us can be dealt with. This will make things like praying and asking for help easier, because we are asking the one who created us and knows how to help us the best. Humbly asking the God of the universe for wisdom - it just does not get any better than that!

Discipline? Who's Got that?

Discipline is one of those words that most of us really hate. It is an interesting word that, while its spelling stays the same, can have different meanings. Here are a few of the definitions: 1) Training to act in accordance with rules. 2) Activity, exercise, or a regimen that develops or improves a skill; training. 3) Punishment inflicted by way of correction and training.

Using these three definitions, here are a few key processes we can implement to help our transformation be more effective and fruitful in our everyday lives. 1) We want to begin to train ourselves to live according to a set of rules or a standard that we set up for ourselves to help keep us on track, on purpose and effective. This calls for a plan! 2) We want to make sure that we do everything in our power to execute that detailed plan, including setting measurable milestones and goals, having people hold us accountable, measuring results and making adjustments where the results are not up to par. 3) We should pay attention and learn from the discipline imposed by life itself. Simply put, we have to make a plan, check on it and tweak it as we go for optimal results. For most successful people, discipline is the thing that gives them the ability to do what is required when they don't feel like it, when they are not motivated to do so and when inspiration has long made its exit.

So the question becomes, how disciplined are you today and what would it take for you to implement a disciplined regiment in your life to make you more effective? This in and of itself is transformation for many of us: to put a plan together! Ask yourself: do you have a schedule that you keep, lists that you write down to ensure you stay on track? Do you have people in your life that help you stay disciplined and accomplish your goal? How do you keep yourself moving forward when there are so many things that can come and grab your attention, take you far to the left of what you want and/or where you planned to be?

I have a few friends who are highly disciplined in their lives. They always seem to be on track. They are the ones who have an excellent workout routine, are seem-ingly able to be everywhere on time, are excellent parents (you know the type - part of the PTA!) and able to get it all done with-out being frazzled. I asked a few of them how they did it. Where did the discipline come from and how did they manage to keep themselves on point? Many gave the same response and it surprised me. They said once they make it a point to do something, they are going to do it no matter how they feel. They all noted they don't let their feelings get in the way once they decide to do something. Once they commit to it, they simply do it no matter what life distraction comes, because they know that feelings are wishy-washy and have a tendency to go in the same direction as our circumstances.

Think about high performing athletes, those who get paid obscene amounts of money to put balls in hoops, cups, through goals, in nets and out of the park. While they seem to have an easy profession and the money seems to be out of proportion with what we would call perhaps more important skill sets (like doctors, teachers or firefighters), they still have to put extra-ordinary amounts of time in to get their skill level to the point where people would pay them for their talent. Those at the highest levels have regimens that they keep no matter what situation comes their way. They know that to perform at a certain level, they have to stay on track and not let themselves slip because they don't feel like training. From what they put into their mouths to how they pamper their bodies, what is certain is that they discipline their bodies to almost work on autopilot so that they get the maximum performance out of it. They hire trainers and coaches to get them going, but there is a mechanism that they have on the inside to push past what appears to be their limitations. Even when the results don't seem like they are optimal, they continue the routine of discipline and work.

Years ago when I was working in Florida on the close-out of building Disney's

Studio Tour Park (I was the financial analyst on some of the rides and shows) I would go to the gym and work out. One day one of the workers asked me to step into the basketball gym but he held his hand to his lips and asked me to be quiet as I stepped in. Once in the gym, I looked down to the other end and saw, of all people, Shaquille 'O Neal practicing free throws. At the time he played for Orlando Magic. To my surprise, he made about 25 in a row and about 40 out of 50 until the coach who was catching and throwing the ball back to him threw the ball too low and it rolled past him and I picked it up. That caused him to notice I was in the room. He said hello and went back to practicing his shots, but began to miss more than he made.

I learned a lot that day about him from watching and talking briefly with him about his upcoming trade to the Lakers. His reputation was (and remained during his career) that he was horrible at shooting free throws. What I knew was that he could shoot them; he just did not shoot them well when people were watching. I also knew that he practiced a lot and with discipline and intentionality. I was impressed with what I saw.

While most of us don't have to be that severe with coaches and high end performances in front of millions, we do need to take a page from their book if we want the optimal performance in our craft, trade and profession. We have to enlist the best coaches and trainers our money can buy to make sure we have a disciplined program that is geared towards whatever transformation we desire. Again, this won't happen on its own. We have to be intentional about what we are doing if we want to see the change that will take us to the next level of our purpose. It won't be easy and it certainly won't be handed to us.

We have to write down a plan. What is written down gets done more often than that which is haphazardly put into the corner of our minds. Writing it down makes it real for many of us. It helps to give a copy to someone else and ask them to hold you accountable to what you want to accomplish. There is a scripture that says write the vision and make it plain so they that read it may run with it (Habakkuk 2:3 paraphrased). Make it plain for your mind, emotions, body and those who would dare to steer you off course. Write it down so you can measure your progress. That which is measurable is most helpful so that you can adjust course if you are not following the plan. Decide that you are going to move past your emotions and do what needs to be done because it needs to be done. You will look up and transformation will be happening according to schedule because you took the time to believe, express it and execute it. Grab a piece of paper and get started today!

Shhh... It's Quiet Time

Moving, running, pressing, shifting, going, pushing, reaching, grinding, determined to get there, wherever there is. Does that sound like you? What is missing from that list? Can you name the missing piece? It may not be so obvious because you rarely think to look for it. I will give you a hint. Words that start with this letter are worth a lot on the scrabble board. Here it is, are you ready? Shhh... It's quiet time! Turn the world off, sit quietly and meditate or pray for a few minutes each day to quiet your mind and your soul and just be in the moment. Difficult to do for some? Absolutely! Necessary for all? Without a doubt. We all need a minute to recalibrate and center ourselves. We need to turn the cell phone off, turn the TV off, get off Instagram, Facebook, Twitter, Periscope, and Snapchat and just let our minds be at peace.

We understand this concept when it comes to kids. We call it a time out or sometimes we actually get the kids to play what we call the silent game. You know what that is, right? You have heard just about all the noise you can stand and you know they are tired or amped up and the only way to survive whatever space you are in is to have them be silent. Why do we feel like we need silence at those moments? Because we are on overload and we have had all our senses can take. Can I tell you that these are not the only times you and I need quiet time? There is simply too much noise grappling for our attention each day; there is hardly any space to think. Quiet time is necessary to reflect, meditate, ponder our lives and decisions, to give deep thought to major decisions, to look back at the decisions we have made and the fruit, good or bad, of these decisions. We need time to be mindful of our lives, give attention to our God and to refresh our minds, bodies and our emotions. Without it, we can be like hamsters on that proverbial treadmill, moving a lot, spending tons of energy but going absolutely nowhere.

For those of you who know God, you already know you need some quiet time to hear His voice. When the volume is up on everything in our lives, it is often very difficult to hear God speaking to us. He does not always come with the big, booming, obvious voice. Sometimes, it is still and small and quiet. In those times, we have the responsibility to intentionally pursue quiet time to just sit and have an attentive ear. That means we have to turn the volume down on the noise makers in our lives, pull away, find some space to be alone and pursue Him. What we can discover in those times is that God not only wants to speak to us, but He also wants to give us peace. It's not the kind of peace we have when it is just physically quiet, but the peace we feel when we are quiet in our minds and our bodies. What peace we often forfeit, all because we don't take things to God in silence.

This is really difficult for me. I have a hard time turning this mind of mine off. In fact, when my daughter was little she would have trouble going to sleep at night. One night after being admonished many more times than I can remember, I went into her room with my lips pressed together and ready to give my mom speech about how she needed to go to sleep. She met me with a very logical and well thought out commentary about how she could not turn her brain off, she could not shut it down and she did not know how to find the switch! I sat there on the edge of her bed a little speechless, groping for words because I knew exactly how she felt. "I cannot find that switch sometimes and I am a grown-up," I thought in silence. But we have to find it; it is imperative for our well-being. It is critical for our pursuit of our passion. It is necessary for our ability to hear from our God.

Now many of you may be wondering who has time for that. Truthfully, we all are given the same amount of time. It comes down to how we prioritize our time. We have to value down-time to reenergize and refresh our mind and emotions. In the stillness of your time you will find that clarity comes back and your creativity is refueled. Perhaps you have noticed that when you don't have adequate time alone to refresh, ideas stop flowing, your patience grows thin and you often find yourself agitated.

A few months ago during my season of being overwhelmed, I was at the grocery store going down an aisle minding my own business. I came to the end of the aisle and a woman was going past the aisle but I could not see her until I saw the front of her basket. It stopped, I stopped but I could not see the person so I moved forward a little only to have this woman snap at me: "Stop your cart - I am passing by!" I stopped quickly and let her pass and apologized. She started fussing at me about not letting her pass and how I was rude. I felt a surge of heat rise up in my face and I had a few thoughts cross my mind for a response and they surprised me. I did not say what I was thinking but apologized again, grateful I have restraint and discipline in my actions. The woman kept fussing but moving forward. I was perplexed about why she was still talking and fussing, but more aware of my deep desire to pop off at her. I did not do it but I wanted to and that needed my attention. Where had my peace gone? It was another sign I needed to pull back and get quiet and recalibrate my life.

So here is the big question regarding this stealth, power move of quiet time: when was the last time you had the chance to hear your own heart beating in your chest? When was the last time you saw the rise and fall of your own lungs from your chest? When was the last time you sat down with a cup of tea or your favorite beverage and read from your favorite book of poetry or favorite author or the Bible? Have you just sat with yourself and taken a moment to rest your soul in the quietness of now, in the silence of nothing? When was the last time you thought about nothing? How about just took a walk in a park or sat at the beach and listened to the waves crash against the shoreline? When was the last time you just listened to the sounds of life around you and thought, "I am alive and I am grateful"? Today would be a great day to do that. If the day has passed, set your alarm clock for 30 minutes earlier and get up and do it first thing in the morning. I promise you will be glad you did. Peace is near my friend.

Detoxing Your Emotions

If you are alive, you are aware of the detox craze our world has taken on. Detoxing used to mean ridding the body of drugs, alcohol or some other life threatening poison that found its way into our bodies. It used to be that you would go to medical facilities to have doctors and professional medical staffs administer this process. Today there are so many detoxing processes and centers that focus on everything from colonics to nasal irrigation to detox diets. By definition, detoxing is a process or period of time in which one abstains from or rids the body of toxic or unhealthy substances. Something toxic is considered poisonous, noxious, deadly or dangerous. In other words, harmful! This can also be called going green, which is a really popular thing these days as well, not just with re-gards to the environment. People are even drinking green things. Perhaps you have joined the craze or seen people taking wheatgrass shots and eating kale.

People are endeavoring to cleanse their bodies of toxins and pollutants so that their bodies run more efficiently. We have gotten a message that our bodies need to be cleansed from time to time of pollutants from our foods and the pesticides that are sprayed on our foods, not to mention the steroids that are fed to the animals to get them to fatten up, etc. We go on Green Tea fasts, we get colon cleanses (can I just put a yuck here?), we do all manner of physical cleanses to get our bodies right so that they run at (what we perceive to be) an op-timal level. The jury is out as to whether this is effective or even healthy but, none-theless, people are detoxing in massive quantities with the hopes that their bodies are better.

Let's go with the premise that detoxing is good for the body and helpful to keep us functioning optimally. Conceptually, the same is equally true of our emotions and our minds. We have just as much coming at us emotionally each and every day. In fact, most of us are on overload emotionally and we do little to make sure that we are emotionally balanced. Think about it: if you transform your life physically, mentally, socially and relationally but emotionally you are still in the same place, it is just a matter of time before all these areas will be contaminated again with the same foolishness you were trying to transform. It is critical that we include emotional detoxing in our process so that we don't get caught sabotaging ourselves and ending up back in the same spot after expending tons of energy.

We need to detox our minds, bodies *and* our emotions from the world's pollutants so that we can efficiently transition to the next without the clutter that takes up space and defiles relationships and businesses. The question becomes: how do we detox emotionally so that we see a real transformation in our emotions and how do we measure the results? First of all, you have to take an emotional assessment of where you are now so that you know when transformation happens. What emotions take up residence inside of your heart the most? Do you struggle with guilt, regret, anger, grief, shame, feelings of failure, not being enough, loss, brokenness, disappointment? Perhaps you find that joy, gladness, hopefulness, confidence, satisfaction, excitement and the like takes up residence in your life most days. Honestly, for most of us it is a combination with the scale leaning in one direction or another. Only you can really know where you land. Looking truthfully at your own emotional landscape is key to knowing how much work you have to do to detoxify yourself and get to a healthy place.

I was counseling a lady once who was sharing her story with me and every description she shared with me was negative regarding how she felt about herself, her job, her marriage, her life and her appearance. The toxicity that ran through her mind and emotions regarding how she felt about herself was enough to jade my perspective about her if I was not careful. The truth was that she was a brilliant, beautiful woman who had hit a tough spot in life, but emotionally she had taken one hit too many in her current career and it had begun to impact her emotional outlook about her whole life. It took a while before I could get her to see that she needed to detox her emotions. I convinced her to take a sabbatical from work for two weeks, change her environment and journal about the future she could imagine without the baggage of her current work space. I gave her some scriptures to meditate on and encouraged her to pick two girlfriends to hang out with during that time that she could be real with and just talk things out. She did that and in about a week she was feeling a little better and in two weeks she was feeling better than that. She was not fully there in the two weeks, but she was on her way. Her transformation was in progress and that was more than she could have anticipated when we got together.

1 John 3:2-3 says, "Yes, my friends, we are already God's children, right now, and we can't even imagine what it is going

to be like later on. But we do know this, that when He comes we will be like Him, as a result of seeing Him as He really is. And everyone who really believes this will try to stay pure because Christ is pure." Even God cares about us trying to live pure lives in every way we can.

The same things don't work for everybody but each of us has to do whatever we can to move the needle for our own lives. Where is the toxicity coming from? Like clearing out our bodies, take the time to fast from whatever is clogging your heart and soul. If people are your parasites, then be bold and courageous enough to let them go. Love them but don't let them weigh your life down. If you are your worst enemy, then get some friends to hold you accountable in how you treat yourself. Make a decision to detox your emotions, your mind and your heart. Go green emotionally! Perhaps it is time to stop by a park and just sit and read a book, pray, talk with a girlfriend, go to the spa, take a nap, go see a counselor, talk to your pastor, whatever it takes. And yes, if necessary, stop by a fruit juice joint and grab a cup of that liquid green stuff for your body - that may even help you clear your mind and let some drama go.

Life Sustaining Self-Care

For a long time, I had the misconception that self-care was synonymous with self-centered and selfish! I did not say this out loud, but it is what I thought internally and here is why: the people who I saw talking about self-care seemed to put an awful lot of emphasis on the *self*-part. I did not see a healthy model of it, but people were constantly telling me I needed to implement it in my life. It wasn't until my body almost broke down due to stress that I realized that there had to be a better way than what I was currently doing. My weight was always looking like a yo-yo due to my hypothyroidism and the stress levels that made the medicine sometimes ineffective. Sleep was what I did when I was too tired to do anything else and eating healthy always seemed to take way more work than just eating whatever was available. Once I crossed the 50 threshold it seemed that everything I had been ignoring the previous 20 years came to sit at my doorstep and I just did not feel well. I wanted to be the best I could be for my kids but I was not demonstrating the best in front of them. I had already made a big declaration that I was not superwoman but my actions said the exact opposite. Something had to give and it was going to be my body if I did not quickly change something.

For me, self-care meant changing doctors to find one who understood exactly where I was at during that point in time. I got a total physical and decided that I was going to do whatever possible to get my mind, body and emotions healthy so that I could feel better and be around to see my beautiful daughters grow into young women. It also meant taking time off and away from all the stressors. It meant realizing that things can run without me and it was prideful to believe that it would fall apart if I was not tending to it, whatever *it* was. It was important for me begin to care about my whole health and make it a priority. I found it was not selfish - it was actually caring about my purpose enough to make sure I was healthy enough to fulfill it.

Not practicing self-care can be almost as debilitating as its nemesis: self-centeredness. Many people have no problem with taking care of themselves at all. In fact, they are experts in paying attention to themselves; they need to care about somebody else for a change. There is a third category as well, and that is those who take care of everyone else and need to be needed. They come off as martyrs with the verbalized intention of getting around to themselves one day. The problem is one day usually doesn't come.

The reason self-care is important can be demonstrated using the analogy of the flight attendant speech we all hear before our plane takes off for its intended destination. Once we have been told the doors have been secured for take-off and we have been admonished for not putting our phones on airplane mode, we are asked to give the attendant in the aisle our attention for the next few minutes. As most of you know, the attendant proceeds to give a demonstration about our seat belts being safely fastened and how the seat cushion can be used as a floatation device in the unlikely case of a water landing. The final piece of information says that in the event the cabin pressure should drop, air masks will drop from the ceiling. The critical piece is this: if you are traveling with a young child or someone elderly or handicapped, please be sure to secure your own mask *first;* then help them put their mask on. Now the reason may be obvious, but I have always felt the need to confirm the obvious. If you don't put your mask on first and for some reason you pass out before securing theirs, both you and they are rendered in-operative. For those of us who are care givers, it is critical that we take care of ourselves because if we don't, we will not be around to help anyone else's life be transformed, changed or turned around for the good.

Today, decide to do self-examination. How are you physically, emotionally and mentally? Are you healthy, are you rested, are you in a position to be around to fulfill your purpose with power? Or are you so exhausted that you are just winging it and responding to what comes at you? If that is the case, it has to end today. What do you need? Is it sleep, a healthy diet, a spa day, a day with your friends doing nothing but hanging out? Whatever it is, make today the day you begin to put your oxygen mask on and take a few deep breaths. It may not look like oxygen is flowing, but I promise soon your lungs, your heart and your mind will appreciate the flow. It is not selfish; it could truly be the most unselfish thing you have done in a long time!

Will the Real You Stand Up?

Before you start any transformation process, it is critical to understand your real identity, meaning who you were created to be and how you want to represent yourself. Society, family, friends and educational institutions will all attempt to tell us who we are, but you were created with a blueprint on the inside preloaded with a plan and a purpose that feels right, flows with grace and fits you. It is imperative that you get a vision of who that person is and focus your plan in that direction so your process is intentional and you end up where you intend to be.

Here is an example: Marcus went to work and everybody there thought he was the funniest guy on the floor. He had them rolling day in and day out. Somebody was always asking him if he was a stand-up comedian afterhours. On weekends at his second job, the team there knew him as serious, on the grind, getting his hustle on and very focused. Seldom did he smile. He did not have time to participate in playfulness. He was on commission at this job and had no time for the foolish jesting he thought they engaged in. If one were to talk to the teammates at the second job, all would agree he was a no-nonsense man with no time to waste. At home, Marcus was responsible but distant to his wife, tender and affectionate to his daughter and son and deeply committed to his mother. His frat basketball team knew him as a fierce competitor who talked trash and the local Home Owners Association wondered how they could get him to voice his opinion at meetings he regularly attended but never spoke up at. Marcus unexpectedly died of a heart attack and at his funeral the varying opinions of his character and who he truly was at heart left everyone scratching their heads and wondering who the real Marcus was.

Do you know people like this? They are one way at work, another at home and someone else at church. Is it you or would people say that about you? Are you so into people pleasing that you change depending on who you are around? Can I share a secret with you? God cares about you and created you just the way you are. In fact, He created you with greatness inside of you! There is no other person like you in the entire world. You are perfect for the purpose for which he created you and no one else can do what He put you on this earth to do. To not be who you are is, in some ways, an insult to the Creator. It is to say that who He created you to be is not enough, it is less than satisfactory, it is somehow less than stellar or that what was created was not good enough and has to be improved upon or needs to be a copy of something else. Truthfully you are enough exactly as you are. Psalms 139:14 says that you are "fearfully and wonderfully made." That, my friend, is a fact.

So how does one get comfortable being themselves? How do you become who you already are and be okay with that and yet transform into a better you simultaneously? Is that even possible? I believe it is possible and I believe you can do it. Becoming who you already are means dropping the facades and allowing yourself to love you! God already loves you dearly and wants to have a relationship with you just as you are. It is true that taking the risk and being the real you simply mean exhibiting trust in yourself and others, being vulnerable and risking being rejected. But the alternative means trying to be what you think others will accept and guessing all the time and playing emotional twister with who you are. You have to settle in yourself that you are not going to please everybody all the time and that is just fact. You have already been accepted by God and that is the most important factor in all of life. Playing it safe is to run the risk of not truly being known and that emptiness is a horrible feeling that no one should live their live with.

Can you accept yourself? Before we look to be ourselves with anyone else, we first have to see if we can be ourselves with ourselves. Can you extend grace to yourself to be yourself? Have a look in the mirror. Go ahead. I will wait.

There you are and you are beautiful, smart and full of potential. You need to embrace that. God has embraced that. Really, He has. You are already accepted so go ahead and accept yourself. Your perceived flaws are part of you and we all have them - they make us uniquely us. This also means that we have to stop giving a lot of credit to what others think and say about us. I will cover this a little later. For now, let's just say you have to know that the trusted voices in your life are the ones that count. Those I call the peanut gallery of life don't count in the grand scheme of things. They make you second guess yourself and worry. Extend grace to yourself and say yes to you. You are worth being loved and that starts with loving yourself. That requires the real you to be present.

Transparency That Makes a Difference

Now here is a word that is tossed out frequently today but it has different meanings to different groups. Everybody talks about being both transparent and authentic, but really most of us are not willing to have the vulnerability that is required to be truly transparent. Let's start with the definition which is having thoughts, feelings, or motives that are easily perceived. Now let's be truthful: how many of you see some people you know in real life whose Instagram accounts hardly reflect the life you know they really live? They look like they are flossin', ballin', styling and profiling but you know that every week they borrow $20 from you until payday (of course). Their profile and real life just don't add up to be the same. This is fake transparency. It is someone showing you their life, but not the real one. I am showing you the one I want to have, dreamed to have, wished I had, but probably won't have. The problem is most of us are not really transparent with ourselves.

Have you ever had someone ask you how you are doing and you decide you are really going to answer them honestly? Then you realize half way through your exchange that they did not really want to know, it was just a greeting. Most of us don't really expect to hear truth. In fact, if you think about it, we discount whatever the person says because we know that they most likely added to it so that it sounds better. We also know that we don't always tell the truth about how life is really going, so we don't expect anyone else to be honest and truthful. We are trying to put our best image out front and we assume that everyone else is doing the same.

How can we expect to reach our goals which require change if we are not really transparent enough with ourselves to know what needs changing? Shakespeare said it best when he said "to thine own self be true." Transparency starts with self. Being honest with ourselves, acknowledging where we really are not, where we hope to be or wish we were. It is one thing to display a fake self to others, but a whole different something to lie to yourself. We are taught to present a particular image from childhood. If we are hurt or abandoned as a child, we learn to not show people who we really are. We learn phrases like "never let them see you sweat" which imply that you should show people only the strong, confident side. That works for some situations, but we all have to let our hair down at some point and be the real us. Sometimes hurting, sometimes jealous, sometimes lonely and often times tired of holding up the fake persona.

While writing, I took a cursory look at Instagram and Facebook and noticed how many entries are about how successful people are implying they are making it happen in their lives. As I looked really close, though, I noticed that much of that was information about their hustle, their grind and in it was a subtle cry for someone, anyone, to see them. See me, hear me, watch me and please, please like me, give me a thumbs up, a heart, something that says you validate me because, after all, I am insecure!

We all want to be seen, heard and respected. That is the basic need of all human beings. However, if we really want to be seen, we have to show ourselves. We can't let being hurt, offended or rejected in the past be a driver for faking the funk in our present. We have to check our motives and be in touch with our real feelings. This is usually not a trait that is taught by our parents or in school while growing up. It is a hard-learned skill that most don't learn unless they put their mind to it.

So who are you really? Not long ago a movie called Divergent came out and with it came many online tests to find out what type of personality you had. The one that everybody wanted was Divergent because it had strong characteristics of all the faction types. The gist of the traits was, Abnegation - the selfless people, Amity - the peaceful, Candors - they were honest, Dauntless – the brave ones, and Erudite - the intelligent group. My kids liked the movie and so we watched it together and afterwards my kids were all guessing that they were Divergent. I thought about the personalities of my children and knew for sure that one was Abnegation, the other was Candor and I thought I was Divergent. The movie website came with an aptitude test that was supposed to help identify which one you were most like. We all took the test and to my surprise, one of my kids turned out to be Dauntless, my husband was Candor and my youngest (true to form) was Abnegation. I did test Divergent, a combination of all the aptitudes which is common for me in many personality and gifts test. What I thought was interesting was how easy it was to guess what some-body else was but for ourselves we picked the one we wanted to be. That is true of most of us in life.

We see ourselves as who we want to be and everyone else who we believe they have shown themselves to be. Indeed, we all are able to see every part of ourselves except our face. We need someone else or a mirror to tell us what we look like at any given moment. This is also true of transparency. It will take the help of *truth* and *honesty* to hold up the mirrors if we really want to be transformed into who we were created to become.

Reaching our goals will take an intentional effort at being transparent with ourselves in order to be successful. Make sure you add some boundaries to your journey. Not everyone is worthy of your complete display of who you really are. In this life, it is necessary to always guard your heart and make sure that you are transparent with those who are receptive to your reveal. Today is as good a day as any to get started. Go ahead, get started. I suggest the first to call are those who will help you the most. Call them up into your life. Truth and honesty are great friends to have in your circle.

Forgiven to Forgive!

You decided you are coming out of this rut and you are making a change but something keeps nagging at the back of your mind, insisting that you are not going to be able to do it. It feels heavy like an anchor tied to your foot; it pulls at you, slowing you down. For the life of you, you can't see what it is that is hanging you up. May I ask you a personal question? Just between you and your journal. What haven't you forgiven yourself for? It may feel like I am prying into your personal life and for some of you I may be missing the mark, but not forgiving is one of the most unsuspected paralyzers of forward progress. Usually we are aware of the things we harbor against other people, but it is often the things we have not forgiven ourselves for that really mess us up and causes tremendous mental blocks.

I get the chance to counsel a number of people in my work as a Transformation Strategist and as an Entertainment/Executive Coach. One common thing I have found is if we have figured out how to forgive others, we have a really difficult time forgiving ourselves. There is one instance where I was working with this really powerful woman and trying to get her business to the next level. She would get to the same place in her business and would plateau over and over again. It was as if she was living out the movie Ground Hog Day. There was this invisible wall that she was not able to scale and she could not see what it was.

We talked for months and finally one day I asked her to tell me about any barriers to her doing whatever she wanted to do in life. She began to share with me that she was doing what she wanted but there were a few things that she could not imagine doing. She knew that there were things in her character that would prevent her based on some decisions she had made before that caused her to draw back. I drew a picture with a wall between her and the things that she wanted to do and then I asked her to write on the wall what those bad decisions were. She did and, as it turned out, she had never forgiven herself for those decisions that had been made early in her career. She had learned from those moves and was much more powerful as a result. I used those things and made steps out of them to climb over the wall. I was able to show her how forgiving herself would release her to grow and find internal peace. This release allowed her to see a future that was not clouded by bitterness, resentment and regret. She had allowed herself to become insecure and second guess herself. Today she is free to dream without the writing on the wall that slows her down and causes her to miss out on greatness. She moves freely without hesitation because she is not hindered by guilt.

To forgive takes courage and humility, plain and simple. It is liberating but takes work to maintain that freedom. All relationships take work and go through a transformation process of their own over time. Walking in the power of forgiveness allows each of us to transform into mature adults in our character, not just in our age and looks. When we choose to forgive we are truly transforming our own lives and the life of the one we are forgiving. We are saying to them, "I think you are worth giving grace to. I am acknowledging that you are human and that you have flaws, but I accept that because I have them and will fail from time to time, as well."

This is not only doable, but must be done if we want to evolve into the powerful and resourceful transformed individual people we want to become. You have to decide that whatever has happened is done and cannot be changed. Forgive yourself for any bad decisions, missed opportunities, wasted time, poor planning, wrong choices of people, fear-based living, or whatever has your mind feeling guilty, embarrassed or ashamed. It is time to let it go and not waste another minute on what you cannot change. Spend time working on that which you can change! Today is here and so are you. Forgive and move forward. More often than not, most everybody around you already has… moved on, that is!

Comfort Zones Destroyed

If any of you have daughters, then you may be familiar with the issues and complexities inherent in the next story I'm about to share and the corresponding emotions that go along with it. One of my daughters, my youngest who is currently 10, wants to be a dancer. As of right now everything is about dance. I would even venture to say that Misty Copeland, the first African-American performer to be appointed as a principal dancer for American Ballet Theatre, is right up at the top of her list under Jesus. YouTube videos, the latest dance moves and everything dance consumes her free time and thought life. Not only does she dance, but she performs in plays. While she would disagree and balk at the very mention of this, she is a really good singer and I believe eventually will fall in the category of a triple threat. Now, I'm not just one of those overly aggressive bragging moms boasting about her daughter. I am for sure not one of those stage moms who think their child is the best of the best and pushes her child up to the front of the line, boasting that her daughter can out sing everyone and should be the star of every play, the lead in every dance ensemble. That's not me. I'm just a mom taking note of her daughter's ability in hopes that she lives up to this potential that I've noticed budding inside of her.

Today, however, was a tough day. At our Community Development Center, we have what's known as a drama consortium. Children from all over the community and those in our church are invited to participate in community plays of the highest caliber. Ms. Pamela Tyson-Mudd, whose résumé extends from Broadway to television to theaters across the globe, has given her time, talent and her vast knowledge to the children in our community. She and her team are excellent at writing plays for the kids, crafting parts that challenge them and stretch them and bringing out the best in each of them. More often than not, she makes them extend past their comfort zone in ways that not only were they not aware they could perform, but their parents were also unaware of the level of talent that was hiding within them. My daughter has been in many of these plays. In one of them she had a key role, playing a star that required her to utilize an Australian accent during the entire play while dancing, rapping, acting and singing.

After taking a break for a season, she went to join the drama team again. To our surprise, after one rehearsal, she decided to quit and not participate anymore. This would have been okay if she had not already given her word, but it was after she was given her part and had committed to being in the ensemble. Here is where parenting can get challenging. The drama director, her dad and I were all in agreement that quitting was not the answer. After asking her a series of questions it was obvious that the only thing that was causing her to want to quit was that she did not feel comfortable because many of her friends were not participating this go-around. You see, her comfort level was connected to her relationships with her friends who were also in the previous plays. We had reached the crossroads where we had to push her past her comfort zone and recognize that what was best for her lay just beyond her ability to see and be comfortable with how things used to be. You can imagine that this did not go over well with our 10-year-old. She fussed, cried, pouted and sulked, but we had to hold our ground. It was important to teach her to push past her perceived limitations and keep her word.

My daughter is 10 and she is still learning how to manage her commitments, her emotions and pushing past her limitations. However, I have found that many of us adults operate below our potential because we love being comfortable and like to live in our familiar comfort zones. We do everything possible to keep it that way. If you are at the top of your game, living at your max potential, earning your maximum income and in the sunset of your life, then comfort is the name of the game. The truth is, most of us are not there yet and so we are not afforded the luxury of staying in the comfort zone all day every day. We are still building; we are still changing, transforming and hoping to see the "more" in us transformed into the maximum performance of us. Comfort can be our enemy if we are not careful. Looking to rest when it is time to press, getting lulled to sleep when we should be studying our craft to be the best we can be. Be careful of contentment when another round of practice will make you better than good. Be careful of getting too cozy with good enough when preparing and being excellent may be the thing that differentiates you from the next candidate.

How do we do this? How do we push past our own comfort zone? First we have to knowledge that what we've been doing so far hasn't been enough. If we can own just this much, we are on the road to pushing into our next best self. We need to recognize that where we are currently in life is

186

not a result of our best efforts, that we want more, that we won't be satisfied until we are more, do more and see more. Once we can admit that we have limited ourselves by what we are comfortable with, we're ready to push past the boundaries that have been self-imposed. Today, decide that you will step beyond that invisible barrier that you have created for yourself. Today, pick one area where you will push yourself into the unfamiliar. Today, write down what might be possible if you have the courage to step out past what those around you are doing and do what you have dreamt was possible for your life. After you write it, take the step. Why wait for tomorrow when today you can begin being what you always knew you could be?

Oh and about that play my daughter was in, well she ended up being one of the lead characters and nailed the part and performed extremely well while having a good time. Isn't that how it usually works? We finally move out of our comfort zone into a place of inconvenience and we stretch ourselves and find that we *can*, we are better than we thought, we are capable of more than we thought. Push, my friends. There is a starring role in the play of your life waiting for you to step up and nail it!

Contagious Confidence

Recently, I went to see an R&B artist from the 90s while in New York. She was a Grammy winner and has some great songs to her credit. My son and I were just hanging out in New York to decompress from months of working nonstop at the church and community development center and we had no agenda other than to have a great time and take it easy. When we came out of the movies and saw the artists' name headlining at a dinner club, we were excited and immediately went to go and get tickets for the upcoming Saturday show. On the day of the show we arrived and found that we were sitting with a gay couple who were incredibly funny and easy to get along with. We immediately knew that no matter what, we were going to have a good time and enjoy the show because of the company we were sitting next to. As the artist started singing, we all noticed that she was not up to par with her usual, smooth vocals that we all had come to know. Sometimes flat, sometimes off key, the artist painfully moved through her set and I felt bad for her. I admit, I get embarrassed for people when they don't perform well and tonight was one of those nights that I knew I would be embarrassed and rooting for the artist to do better so that the people would not complain or feel like they did not get their money's worth. I don't know why that is important to me when it isn't me, but I care.

It was clear that the struggle was real. The artist began to cover other singer's songs that were in a lower register while the audience simply wanted to hear the songs she was known for even if they did not sound like they did when she was in her twenties. It got so tight in there that she even mentioned a few times that she would need help from the audience and proceeded to spend a great deal of time having the audience sing the songs for her. As the evening went on I thought to myself, "She is losing her confidence." With each bad note and the silence of the audience the artist began to become less and less confident. She did not even want her background singers to out sing her and said as much! I wanted to take a needle and inject confidence from my seat. I wanted to yell "You've got this!" I wanted to go on stage and take her to the side and encourage her and let her know they came to see her and hear her music. "Sing your songs!" I wanted to scream. "Don't draw back or shrink, just be you. We know you are in your 50s now, so are most of us who came to see you!" I wanted her to know she could still stand with confidence.

Has this ever happened to you? You lose your confidence at a time when you really needed it. Truthfully, most of us could use a bigger dose of confidence every now and again. It is those times when we perform at our worst or make a mistake that others are aware of that we begin to lose our swagger. Can I tell you that it happens to everyone at some point or another and it is not the end of the world? It is those times when we are feeling a little insecure that we need to stop, reassess what we are doing and regroup. It is then that we need to tell ourselves we were born for this. We have to remind ourselves that we are capable of pulling it off, and even though it may not be on 10, it will be enough. To know that you are enough is powerful. To know that you can do something will cause you to actually be able to reach the goal. "Life and death are in the power of the tongue" (Proverbs 18:21) is an incredible scripture that holds true because we end up believing what we say about ourselves.

While processing through a decision to make an area of your life more productive or change a part of you, be sure you don't let your confidence dip. It is tempting to look around you while dismantling yourself and see people who appear to be whole and completely put together and then get discouraged. It is important to not compare yourselves with others during your process of change. Might I add that social media is not helpful during a transformation process. If you take your eyes off your purpose and begin to focus on what others are doing you will find that you will get off track. Your body will go where your eyes go, so keep your eyes on the direction you are supposed to be moving in. Social media makes us think that everybody is doing amazingly well. People tend to put high-lights and great success on social media. They don't tend to put defeats, depression, lost jobs, divorces, failures, bad days or even their own transformation process on there until they are complete. You know what I am talking about, the famous "be-fore" and "after" picture. They don't just put the before. They only show the belly out after the belly is gone. So be careful that your confidence does not take a hit while you are transitioning through this cy-cle and working on yourself.

Make sure that you don't inadvert-ently sabotage yourself by comparing your-self to everybody around you and believing that you are the only broken one or the only one who is not 100% together. Trust me, everybody has things to work on and if they say they don't, they need to work on dealing with truth and reality. I encourage you to check your courage quotient. How confident are you to keep pushing in spite of setbacks and delays? If you are lacking confidence, take the time to write down your blessings and good traits, note your successes and all the times that you thought you were not going to make it only to later see that you pulled through. Note how you were made better as a result of the adversity and allow your confidence to be built up and encouraged. You are powerful, you are strong, you have made it this far, you will make it the rest of the way. You can be confident because before the world was ever formed you were created to accomplish great things. Get to stepping, push forward. You are confident and you are powerful... let them see it, come on, let it out, it will be okay, I promise. Others will be better because you dared to let your confidence be at the forefront of who you are.

Trusted Voices

Do you remember when you were growing up and there were people in your life who you automatically listened to? Whether it was the tone of their voice or the fact that they cared, something about them made you pay attention, made you give them your ear, made them trust their voice in your life. Trusted voices in our lives are invaluable. When in transition, moving from wherever we are to a better place, we need trusted voices to speak in the dark spaces when we can't quite see our way to the next step. It is those voices that help us navigate the terrain and keep our confidence steady when our footing is unsure. These voices need not be experts, they don't have to speak daily, they don't have to be old or young, and they don't have to be of a particular gender. They simply need to be able to be trusted. Trust is important because when you need to hear advice, encouragement or wisdom, it is usually in a moment where having to hesitate or evaluate the integrity of the giver corrupts the moment and causes undue pressure and stress. The art of cultivating relationships that lend themselves to speaking into one another's lives is a worthy endeavor. I say the "art of" because it takes paying attention to who is in your ear and the fruit of those conversations to determine whose voice it is you should trust and when. Likewise, when it gets really balanced, you find that you also become that voice to those in your sphere of influence. Today you may need that trusted voice of encouragement, but tomorrow it may be your friend who needs to draw from your well. It is a sad scenario when we don't have people who can hear the discouragement in our voice or see the dim flicker of light in our eyes or who don't notice we have dropped out of community for a while. That is a lonely and sad day and, believe me, many people find themselves in that place.

For years I longed for a mentor, a spiritual mom of sorts, someone who would truly know me and my patterns and have the wisdom and experience to speak to me in times of trial and decision making. I was blessed with one right after my 46th birthday. I was so excited and elated that I finally had someone I could talk to and who would push me to be my best with no agenda. As is typical of most relationships, she did not start out as a trusted voice but an expert voice that I trusted because of her position and knowledge. I make this point on purpose because sometimes we find trusted voices in places we do not intend or expect to find them. My mentor started out as my therapist, a paid consultant to help me off-load and navigate my way through the heavy burden of my profession. However, because I made a commitment to be open and vulnerable, the relationship took off and became one of my most valued and treasured connections. Through the course of a couple of years as I specifically and intentionally opened up to listen with my whole self, she gave of herself without hesitation. That relationship became the most stable and critical to my heart, emotions and other relationships. It was an incredible journey, filled with self-discovery, correction, encouragement and wisdom beyond my wildest imagination.

I wish I could tell you that it was a forever relationship, but sometimes trusted voices are in our lives for a season and no more. Sometimes they are for a specific set of circumstances or for a particular lesson. In my case, that relationship sadly only lasted 3 ½ years due to cancer. I have to be transparent and honest here: I did not understand why God would give me something so amazing only to have it snatched out of my life so quickly. It took me a while to understand that she was gone but her lessons and wisdom lived on in me and through me in my speaking and teaching. I came to realize that every trusted voice is not a forever voice, so make the most of it, take the time to appreciate it and take it all in. Never take for granted people you value and love. Let them know from your own lips while they are alive how much you care. Life can hurt us but if we let ourselves trust and take it in, those voices will continue to speak from graves and crypts. Their wisdom and counsel will guide you for years to come.

One thing this particular relationship taught me was that I really did need those voices and they are critical to help me truly see myself and how I may be perceived by the world. Remember from earlier, the one thing we can't see with our eyes is our own face. You need someone else or a mirror to see your face. Trusted voices in our lives, whether old or young, social friend or professionals, help by sharing what they see in us and help us when we shift off our patterns and act out of character. Do you have a trusted circle of friends or a mentor, someone you trust to tell you when you are wrong and to encourage you when you are down? Are you teachable enough to have others speak into your life or do you perceive yourself to be someone who has it all under control? I pray you are the former and realize that there is so much more to life than that which we know. Some younger know more about certain subjects and some older, but in both directions there is knowledge to be gained.

As I said earlier, you may be in a season where you may need that trusted voice of encouragement - don't worry, seasons don't last forever. Tomorrow you may have to draw from your well and speak life to someone who trusts you. That is what makes trusted relationships so special. They can be mutually beneficial and powerful. Trusted voices are a necessary part of the transformation process. None of us make it alone and, while we need the quiet and the silence, we also need the call of one who can say "I see you." How about reaching out to someone you know needs a call or a touch? Sow the seed; you will draw from that deposit one day. That, my friend, is a part of life.

The Infamous "They"

Have you ever started a new process and found that everyone had an opinion about it? People come out of the walls talking about the time they did whatever it is that you are now doing. They have stories and testimonies about how they did it and how it worked or did not work for them. More often than not, the stories are how the process, gizmo, gadget, or situation did not work for them. I am not sure what compels people to want to tell of their experiences, oftentimes to complete strangers and without provocation, but it is true they do and sometimes it is difficult to get them to shut up. Let's not even talk about when you are about to get married or, worse yet, pregnant! Those are bad enough, but the real culprits who get to us are those who criticize us and share opinions about us and our character to others, the ones who somehow garner our attention and make us believe they have weight and authority regarding our worth. They have managed to get into our heads and established a place of influence even though they have not given birth to us, are not responsible for our welfare and in no way provide for our day to day living.

My point here is people will always have an opinion about what you are doing - good or bad. I call them the infamous "they." "They" have an opinion about everything, "they" talk about everybody, "they" seem to know everything but pay for nothing, "they" judge everyone but can't seem to be held accountable because no one really knows who "they" are. The real question is why do we listen to them? We wonder what "they" think over and over again. We give energy, thought and emotion to people who may or may not really care about our well-being or our destiny. What do they think about what I am wearing, who I am dating, where I go to school, what I drive, what my kids look like, what they do, how I am aging, am I sexy, do I look old, am I beautiful and are they talking about me? We spend so much energy wondering what they think. As my grandmother use to say, "They don't pay any of your bills and can't get you into heaven or keep you out of hell!"

Last week my daughter came into my office after school and she looked a little down. After some motherly quizzing, trying desperately to not overstep those invisible boundaries that send teenagers spiraling back into their caves, I got her to share with me what was troubling her. She said she had a bad day because a good friend of hers was dating someone that she thought was bad for them and she had to look at them all day at school. Everywhere she went there they were, cuddled up, and it drove her crazy. She said it literally ruined her day. Her friend had called her over as they noticed her not acting her usual cheerful way. She said they told her not to be mad and just be happy and then went over and hugged their partner. She wanted to throw up and it made her really angry. I said I was sorry for her having a bad day and I prayed that tomorrow was better. Her response caught me off guard and made my heart hurt for her. She said she hoped it was but that would depend on if she saw them and if they were coupled up! Wow, that got me. One, because she is my daughter. Two, because I realized her joy, peace, and emotional well-being were being determined by someone else. I sat there and I tried not to overreact but I wanted to give her some wisdom on how this situation would lead to a lifetime of allowing people and situations to dictate her emotions and tone for the day. I asked her if I could share with her a bit of an allegory type of dialogue to help communicate what I was thinking.

I told her that each day she woke up with a bucket of clear water that was her source to draw from daily. Each morning when she woke up, she and God could determine if drops of joy and peace would be put into the water or she could give the power to someone else to decide what would go in the water. By giving the power to someone else, she was giving control of her emotional state to someone else. She had to live with whatever they put into the bucket. If it was rejection, sadness, loneliness or boredom, she had to live with it because she gave them control over her emotions for the day.

Her worth, her value was now in the hands of someone else. I proceeded to let her know that she was way too valuable, smart, brilliant and beautiful to give someone control over her day, her heart and her emotions. She listened intently and said she understood. I let it go after that. I thought that was enough mom stuff for one day and just prayed she really did get it.

Even adults need to heed the same advice. We wake up with the ability to have joy and peace and a day filled with happiness and worth. Why let people who don't know you for real in the first place speak words that tear you down and chip away at your confidence? More often than not, it isn't about you in the first place. They are really trying to make themselves feel more important and the only way to do that is to put you down a little lower so they feel a little higher. If we are going to move to the next level and live a transformed life in a place where our dreams come to pass, we have to stop listening to the haters and listen to that still small voice that speaks life to you and lets you know that you were created for greatness. I recommend you ignore them and realize you will never please "them" anyway. If you are going to give thought to anything then let Philippians 4:8 be your guide: "Finally, brothers and sisters, whatever is true, whatever is noble, whatever is right, whatever is pure, whatever is lovely, whatever is admirable—if anything is excellent or praiseworthy— think about such things." That will change your mindset! You can live your life everyday knowing that you have already been accepted by the one who matters most

(Ephesians 1:6) —the one who created you. What others think is only relevant if YOU think their opinion is important, so be careful to whom you give that power.

Dangerous Distractions

Dangerous distractions come in many forms and packages. They come in luxury models, bargain priced distractions, sexually enticing prototypes, and full on Hollywood staged production-sized distractions! Whatever your pleasure, there is a distraction tailor-made for you. Have you noticed that as soon as you decide you are going to change something in life the distractions come from the East, West, North and South? Old boyfriends or girlfriends come back around, even married ones. It is the weirdest thing, but trust me on this, you cannot afford to be taken off track. Time is critical at this moment. You have to ask yourself how much you need this transformation at this moment in time. Go ahead. Ask yourself right now. How important is it to you? Do you want it? Do you want it bad enough to change your life, change your circumstances, change your circle, change your attitude, change your routine? If yes, you have to get to a place where you manage the distractions that come your way and prevent you from your God-ordained destiny.

So what exactly qualifies as a distraction? It could be anything that keeps you from focusing on what you should be giving your full attention to. It does not have to be something important and it does not have to keep your attention for long. There is a major campaign going on right now about texting while driving. Most of us are against texting and/or making calls while driving and we shake our heads in feigned disgust when it is mentioned. But, if we are really honest, most of us are just a little bit guilty of it and some of us are regular of-fenders. That chime goes off and we are addicted to its pull. It is as if the president himself is calling us personally. We don't consider that even a split second distrac-tion could easily cause us to be staring at our maker in the next second.

I have a 10-year-old and right now she is the queen of distraction. The number of distractions between downstairs and go-ing upstairs to clean her room is about 927! It is amazing to me how she can find so many things to occupy her mind between those two destinations. Adults are no dif-ferent. We know that we need to make some adjustments in order to transform our lives, but somehow we get sidetracked with every little thing that has nothing to do with our intended destination. Destiny is calling. Not only are there distractions in the way, but some of them are dangerous because they are the kind that not only steal time, but they steal energy and purpose.

Have you ever met people who had so much potential in them and you knew they were just a tweak or two away from greatness, but they let one distracting left turn cause them to veer off into an abyss and they never ever got back on course? How about this, have you ever been moving in a direction and took a break to look at one thing and that led to something else and then something else and before you know it you are no longer on course? You don't even remember what you were doing! Do you know people who said they were going to take one semester off from school to make just a little money and got distracted with a low level job and never went back to school to finish the degree? Do you know people who met someone who was not the right person for them but somehow got distracted by one inconsequential but desirable trait that they liked and before you know it had a baby and then another one and felt stuck and then life settled in and they were miserable? These are examples of distractions that are dangerous because they change your course of life. You have too much to do, there is too much in you, and there are too many people waiting on your arrival for you to get hung up chasing the wind. You have a purpose to fulfill and you can't do it being distracted with foolishness.

When you decide to embrace transformation you have to do it with a distraction buster gun in your hand. You can't be derailed by rabbit trails that lead to nowhere. Staying focused and committed will get you to your goal. Be like the race horse that has those blinders on so that they can only see in front of them. They are designed so that the horse cannot see to the left or right and they can't see the competition or what is behind them. All they can see is the road ahead and it keeps them focused on the finish line and in tune with their rider's directions and instructions. Proverbs 4:25 says, "Let your eyes look directly forward, and your gaze be straight before you." In other words, don't get distracted with the unimportant. It may be important at another day and time, but in this season it does not fit! That also means we have to pay attention to what we do, who we are around and what is occupying our minds. I will tell you that for many of us the *distraction du'jour* is social media. We wake up checking Facebook, Twitter and Instagram before we get out of bed. If we are not careful, we can let not just minutes go by, but hours as we troll the feed looking at what others have supposedly accomplished while our day slips away. We have to keep our goal in sight and in tuned with our Creator's directions. He has a plan and our steps are ordered daily. It is wise to not pay attention to the left or the right and instead focus on our next step towards our intended purpose.

So today, square your shoulders and make a decision to keep your gaze on the prize in front of you - the transformed you. Come on, say it with me: "I am changing. I am becoming the best me I can be." Yes, I know it feels funny to say it out loud, but I need you to hear it out of your own mouth with your own words and I need you to believe it. Become the YOU that you were created to be. You are powerful and you are a force and you have a designed purpose that was planned out before you were even born and you must keep that date with destiny.

You have no time to be distracted, not to-day, not tomorrow, and not ever. You are being transformed for purpose, on pur-pose, by purpose.

What Do You Believe?

This next power move impacts all the others and makes an impression on just about everything you do. This is your belief system. Everybody has one, even those who claim they don't believe in anything. Your belief system is critical if you want to successfully move through a transformation process with purpose, on purpose and ultimately fulfill your purpose. Please trust me when I tell you one more time, you are most successful, most efficient and most satisfied when you are operating in what you were created to do. What you believe about yourself, who you believe in greater than yourself, and what you *believe* you can achieve in this short but powerful life of yours will determine what you can *actually* achieve. It sounds corny, but it is really true: if you can see it, you can achieve it. If you can believe it, you can receive it. So many of us fail because we simply don't believe we can reach the goals we have set for ourselves and so eventually we stop setting them. There are people you know right now who don't believe in themselves, don't believe in God, don't believe in much of anything and they are miserable because having faith is a huge part of life. Even if you don't believe you have any, we all were given a measure of faith by our Creator according to Romans 12:3.

Beliefs are critical because they determine our behavior. What you believe will govern how you act and that will determine where you go and what you do when you get there. Some beliefs are religiously based and some are morally based. We all have them and they are shaped by our experiences, our culture, our families, etc.

How you see yourself and how you value yourself will determine how far you are able to move up into the next level of life. What you believe about how you fit and your importance makes a real difference. If you don't believe you are worth anything, others will confirm it. However, when you know your worth, it really doesn't matter what others think. If you are not treated with the respect and appreciation you believe you deserve, it may mean people are unaware how much you are worth based on how you allow them to treat you or how you talk about yourself.

Accepting their inferior treatment means you are adjusting who you are to match what they think, and maybe confirming what you think, as well. In their mind, this gives them the right to devalue you, both mentally and emotionally. Over the course of time, you will have trained them in this behavior. If you don't value yourself, they are no longer required to do so.

One example I can share is of a lady named Octavia. She was a beautiful young woman but grew up a middle child with a really talented older sister and a sickly younger brother. Her parents loved her deeply but did not have a lot of time for her because of her brother's needs and her sister's modeling career that demanded her "momager" constantly run around with her older sister. Octavia felt she had to tend to herself and attend school events alone. Slowly but surely she began to stop asking for attention and came to the conclusion that she simply was not important enough for love.

As she entered high school, she did not believe people when they complimented her on her looks or talents. She thought that they were patronizing her and so she shrugged it off. When boys began to take notice of her, she ignored their request for dates, as she thought they were asking to simply make fun of her because she truly believed that she was not beautiful. Her father had jokingly said that she was not the "pick of the litter!" He had no idea that his word set in like quick forming concrete in her already insecure mind. Octavia's belief about herself was that she was unwanted and unloved and so she projected this thinking to everyone who dared to come close.

As time went on, Octavia graduated from high school with good grades and enrolled in a local state college. She finished her degree in business and got an average job in an accounting firm, but in her was a feeling that greatness was somewhere in there. However, fear that she was not enough kept her from lifting her head to see it or pursue it. Those around her saw sparks of potential in the smallest things she did, for they were done with excellence, integrity and attention to detail like nothing anyone had ever seen. Although many tried to encourage her to find out what her true passion was, she would always deflect the questions to the side because somewhere in her she had settled on the fact that she was not worthy of anything great happening to her.

As a result, her bosses stopped trying to promote her and she began to languish at her jobs. One after the other she would stagnate because she received the same energy she gave them. They bought what she was selling. She was not worthy of promoting, not worthy of advancing, not worthy of paying attention to. One day she met a new co-worker at her latest job who had overcome incredible odds to land the job with their company. As they talked at lunch and exchanged stories of their lives, Octavia realized that her upbringing was pretty fairytale-ish compared to her new friends. She asked her friend what made her decide to overcome all of these things and be happy and love and pursue her dreams and really live. Octavia's friend answered that she had to decide to believe in something greater than herself. There had to be more in this life than what she was seeing and so she decided to stop believing in just what she saw and believe in the Creator. She decided to believe in the plan the Creator had for her life and follow it. That day revolutionized Octavia's life. Something in that sparked the greatness that was dormant inside of her and a movement towards transformation started. To be a part of something greater than herself and to be transformed by the one who created her sounded intriguing and liberating.

That day she made a decision to believe. It didn't happen overnight, but step by step she got to know the one who gave her life and she got to know herself and the changes that were required to become who she was designed to be were permanent. One day she looked up and so did everybody else and there was a new person there who had light in her eyes, joy in her soul, purpose in her step and a passion for life that included inspiring those around her to live in the moment with a mission that was effective and intentional.

What do you believe and are you holding true to your beliefs? Are they working for you and is one of those beliefs that you were created with purpose in mind? What are you doing to stay true to your belief system? If you don't have one, there is a Creator who longs to love you and show you a life that you never knew possible: not rules and regulations but love and possibilities. Today is the best day to transform your life from one that may be wandering aimlessly to one that is intentionally moving in a direction. Sit for a minute and think about it. What do you believe and is it authentic, real and powerful? If so, let it lift you. If not, you have some work to do so get started today!

Something's in My Eye

"Have a vision. It is the ability to see the invisible. If you can see the invisible, you can achieve the impossible." ~ Shiv Khera

Do you have a **vision**, a vision for your life? Where do you see yourself in five years or ten years? This is an important question to ponder. Maybe you have heard R. Kelly sing, "If I can see it, I can be it" or the Bible verse in Proverbs 23:7, "As a man or woman thinks in their heart, so are they." So the question is, what do you see? What is the plan for your life today and in the days to come? What do you want to do and be? What is the plan for that vision? Do you see the new transformed you, unstuck, happy, and filled with joy, helping others, financially fit, spiritually grounded, emotionally balanced, and soaring professionally? Or are you stuck and can't see beyond the kids crying and screaming, your husband asking where his underwear is, your wife complaining that you don't do enough? Is it that report that is due in the morning that you have not started, that project that you've been meaning to do for 5 years, that 26 ½ pounds you need to lose as you throw down that whole bucket of Blue Bell ice cream at 1 am? Do you see yourself being in another wedding and having to shell out money for a dress you will only wear once and shoes that hurt your feet from the time you put them on? Is there another person asking you if you have anyone special in your life and you making up a fake answer when you know you have not been on a good date in the last 2 years? What do you see? You say: "Well, did you have to go there?"

We fool ourselves way too often but I think if somebody just says what everybody is thinking, it helps us know we are not alone in our struggle. It helps us know we are not crazy and that other people around us are asking the same questions that we are: "Is there more than this to life? Will I ever get to be the person I know lives on the inside but is buried under this mound of stuff that I did not even plan to have in my life?" We all have a list that we have to adjust and transform so that we can see what we need to see, and that is the man or woman who is flowing in purpose, living in reality but moving towards destiny. We each want to be a person who is living out their passion while pursuing the boundaries of more than we could have ever expected of ourselves and inspiring others around us to live out their dreams in

238

ways previously unimaginable.

So can I tell you something that you may not want to hear? You are currently living out the previous vision you had for your life in days gone by. Yes, it is true. Decisions you made yesterday are impacting your life today and decisions you make today will impact you tomorrow. Likewise, how you envisioned your life to be yesterday is how you are living today. So we have to change our vision today so that our future is what we want it to be. How do we get our vision rightly aligned, our internal ideologies and our action plan for transformation moving in sync with one another? I am so glad you asked that question! First, you have to start with some thought. Real thought, quiet, intentional meditative thought about who you are and what you believe God put you here on earth to do and be. Not what your parents want, not

239

what your boo wants or what you want to be to show up that kid who lived down the street who was always good at everything.

After you have sat with that for a while and know it to be true, write down the vision for your life on paper. There is nothing like having a picture of what you want to achieve in this life over time to inspire you and keep you focused. It becomes your guiding point for measuring where you are at intervals of five, ten and twenty year points.

Write the vision plainly and put it somewhere you can refer back to it. You may even want to make a vision board; put it in your phone or on your bathroom mirror. Just make sure you look at it and make adjustments as it becomes clearer in your heart and mind. Bruce Lee said, "A goal is not always meant to be reached, it often serves simply as something to aim at."

Sometimes our vision may seem too lofty, but let it be and push for it. I promise you aiming for it is not a sin or a crime and only the haters will be mad if you reach it.

So today I challenge you to take the first step in moving towards the YOU I see you to be. Yes, I see you. "How?" you ask. Well, you have gotten this far in reading this book and if that is the case, you are serious about transforming your life and becoming better. I see that you can and will change and become the best you. I believe you have been making some life altering changes and they are showing up in your life. My commitment has been to pray for every person who chooses to pick up a copy of this book and dedicate themselves to purpose and transformation, so I know you are changing and moving towards greatness because I know God answers prayers! Take some time today and the rest of this week to visualize the new you. See yourself doing what you have been called to do. Visualize it, verbalize it and compose it on paper and then put action to it and watch it begin to materialize in your life!

Awake to Dream Again

When was the last time you dreamed and did not limit yourself or pull back your **dream** because it seemed too outlandish or out there? Remember when you were a child and you would dream and unabashedly share your dreams with anyone who would listen? What happened to us so that we not only stopped sharing our dreams, but we actually stopped dreaming? "When I grow up, I'm going to be an astronaut, no… wait umm a, a, pilot, then a singer, then after that I'm going to be a professional athlete, then I am going to play in a band and buy buildings and own this whole block!" Does this sound familiar? If your friends were like mine as kids, that is how we used to talk. We would say things like that as if we were going to have 10 differ-ent lives all in one because we were dream-ing and thought it was all possible. There were no limitations because we had suf-fered no setbacks yet, no one had poured water on our dreams, no one had told us no, no banks had rejected our loan re-quests, we had not lost any jobs, we had not failed at a business or flunked a class in college. It was all fair games at that point because the sky really was the limit, and even then the sky was limitless because we could see no end to it, either. Failure was not in the equation. Life had not happened to us yet. Dreaming was free and we could do it at our leisure and until our hearts were content.

Guess what? Dreams are still free. Fear is what costs us, and it is expensive. It costs us time, energy, emotion, lost op-portunities and it steals our dreams. Yes, I know that the economy has caused many dreams to go belly up and jobs are hard to find, the housing market has made having a home to sleep in and dream in difficult, but truthfully, starting over is still possible and it starts with dreaming about it. What does this take? It takes courage. Why courage? When we have had dreams before and it seems like they have not come to pass, we get fearful that if we try again we will encounter the same result, but that does not have to be true. One of the chapters in this book is about transparency and so I will share a little about my journey for a second. I am one of those people who have visions, and I mean big visions. Compared to some I have accomplished a lot and compared to others nothing. The comparison though is not to anybody; it is to the plan I believe God has laid out for my life. I believe I have so much more to do it can be overwhelming and daunting sometimes. I have many dreams, goals and aspirations and oftentimes I see my life clock and it appears to be ticking faster and faster as the days go by with no fulfillment in sight.

From time to time I can get to the point where I don't want to dream anymore because the dreams I have not come to pass, but my options are these: give up and live hopeless and miserable the rest of my days or fight through the discouragement and find the courage to dream again, in spite of what the circumstances may be. The time is going to pass anyway. I can be found courageously pushing towards the vision that has been given or floundering as a victim of life's blows. I choose to fight and am determined to win. The odds are on my side. There is a chance I can dream, get vision, put action to the vision and be victorious. If I quit, there is no chance of winning. I have won before and I have quit before, so I know what both are like. I think winning feels better. Dreaming costs, me nothing but courage. I just have to pull it up over my fear of failure because it is in me and it is in you. We just have to decide to dream again. It is worth the effort. You know it and I know it and the opposition knows it. So let's quit playing around and get to it.

There was this guy in the bible named Joseph. His story is found in Genesis around Chapter 37. He is famous for having dreamed an incredible dream and sharing it with his family. Unfortunately, because the dream spoke about him reigning over his family, they were not too excited about it and decided that they would not only kill the dream but also the dreamer. This story happens a lot in life and if we are not careful we will share our dreams with people who are insecure or don't know their own purpose so yours intimidates them. Read the story when you get a chance, but eventually exactly what Joseph dreams comes to pass. It is this very scenario that saves his family and allows them to live through a devastating famine. Joseph's story reminds us that not everyone is going to agree with your dreams and some will even try and stop you, but you are unstoppable. You can achieve what you dream to do if you don't give up and quit or let others convince you that they are not worth pursuing. You have work to do and really it is about the people you have been called to impact. You are gifted for purpose. The transformation that is forthcoming will blow people's minds and bless them beyond belief. I challenge you to dream bigger than you ever have before and see that not just your own life will be blessed by the changes that are being birthed in you, but also the lives that will be touched by your talent, your touch, and your presence. Let your dreams flow freely so that you can see the breadth of your reach. This is bigger than you!

Dreams are our imaginations being unleashed to explore past the boundaries of what seems impossible. Here is the question: if there were no limits, what would you dare to do? Come on, think! If you did not have restrictions of resources, time, age, gender, race, religion, family responsibilities, education or skill, what would you do? Is that a smile coming across your face? Are you starting to remember? Remember what it was like to hear yourself say, "I would be..." Today, for just a moment in your quiet time, dream and journal about how it felt to be a kid.

Let yourself find the courage to let the fear go of past dreams not being fulfilled. That is over and gone. Today is a new day and this is a new dream season. I would be willing to bet that some of the dreams that you think are long gone are not dead, just lying dormant. No fear, new courage, maybe old dreams but a new you with a new plan. Let's go.

One Step at a Time

At my church we are having a baby boom. I mean a real boom. Every other week someone is coming up to me whispering in my ear "I am pregnant!" In the past three years we must have had over 20 babies born and now we are on the second round. The reason this is such a big deal is we started off as a church full of college students 12 years ago. In the aisles you would most likely trip over a back pack in those early days. Now you walk down those same aisles and the ushers are asking people to move their strollers. It is absolutely wonderful. One of the by-products of having so many babies born is we have toddlers who are everywhere and one at a time we are watching them learn how to walk.

Everybody knows that **one step at a time** is how we teach babies to walk. They don't really walk first; they simply learn to take a step. Usually around nine months to a year or so after they have mastered crawling and pulling themselves up with the help of furniture, they stand and learn to balance and then try to take a step. They don't run first. Just one simple step and we all go crazy. In fact, they fall countless times before they actually master that step and we all think that is okay and we applaud their falls because they tried and we want them to try again. Eventually they get that step down, then another and they walk. It is only later that we long for the days when they could only crawl as they get into all the cabinets and out of their cribs!

There are other areas of life this principal comes into play as they grow up. How about math? We don't just throw them into calculus! One level at a time is how we teach our kids addition, subtraction, multiplication, division and so on. Line upon line, here a little, there a little, we teach them. Somehow we grow up and all of a sudden we want to skip levels and combine steps to get to the end quicker. There are no shortcuts in life. I know that we see people on TV and social media and people look like overnight successes, but we don't really know how long those people have been grinding. Even people on shows like *The Voice* and *American Idol* have a background story that shows they have been bartending, teaching at preschools, working at the airport and doing all kinds of jobs while trying to figure out what the next step is to fulfilling their dreams. There are steps to everything, even when it looks like it should be right within our reach.

Patience is the key here, and staying the course and even trying to enjoy each step. What is the advantage of really paying attention to each step along the way? There is something wonderful to be learned at each station in life. If we take our time, allow all of our senses to be engaged, our eyes, our ears, our sense of smell, our mind and our heart, we will get so much more out of the journey. I want to encourage you to try to take each step with the mindset that your transformation is dependent upon on a complete and thorough investigation of each particular stride. If you try to do too many steps at a time, things will get over whelming and you won't know what is causing you angst. I have a saying that goes, "When too many variables are changing simultaneously, it is difficult to solve for y." You remember that from algebra in school, right? Well it is true of life, not just math!

In general, anytime we start assessing our lives and checking to see what we want to change, it is important we understand that we can't do it all at once. That will be too overwhelming and perhaps cause us to give up, as it will weigh heavily on us and feel as though there is no way to change so many things. So when we talk about allowing our life purpose to be the push we need to transform our lives, we need to keep this practice in mind. You have to get your focus goggles on, put some good music on and get ready to step up to the plate for a great ride. I am talking about one amazing power move at a time. Let that one thing be the center of your attention until that phase is sufficiently complete. It will be easier to measure progress and have some satisfaction that things are moving forward when you have a specific area you are working on.

Finally, one step at time insinuates that there are multiple steps in a progression, the subject of our next chapter. Here we are isolating the step, but it is part of a larger picture which is the process itself. Each step builds upon the other, which is also why it is critical that you finish the steps. It is sort of like a puzzle. You need all the pieces for the whole picture to be complete. You can't throw away a piece because it looks boring or like another piece. All the pieces are important and distinct, even if to the natural eye it looks almost exactly like the piece next to it. The nuances that it possesses are important to the overall picture and make for the completing and solving of the puzzle. Put the piece in its proper spot and you will feel motivated and experience a sense of accomplishment as your list begins to decrease and your full, purposed picture comes into view.

Come on my friend, take stock of where you are and where your next step needs to be; then pick your foot up, put one foot in front of the other, one-step at a time, my friend. Soon you'll be walking out the door!

Trust the process!

Ok you have to do me a favor before we get into this transformation power tool. You have to put your faith hat on. Already before I type the chapter I can feel in my spirit this one is going to be tough. The words that are coming to my mind are words we simply don't like. Even in the title of the chapter I think I heard you gasp. Trust is a scary word for some and process... well, I almost lost half of you right there. Put them in the sentence and then say we are going to devote a whole chapter to them and something does not seem to be right in the world in that moment. Truthfully, every process has to be trusted if it is going to be effective.

Trust is hard and many of us are still

in therapy trying to get over our trust issues. But trust that if God has you in a process of humility, or waiting, or working something out of you or trying to teach you, then you will be better off after you get the lesson. That is guaranteed. The efficacy of the intended outcome is predicated upon the fact that if you work the process to its fullest and do what is required, the desired outcome will occur. Trust is required to believe that. Did I just add another word? I think I did. You have to not only trust, you have to *believe* that the process will deliver on its promise for the intended outcome. Whew, this is asking a lot, isn't it? Yes, my friend, it is.

It is true that in any process we go through, personal development or otherwise, we will be tempted to distrust that the process is working. There are many reasons for that: the slowness of the process itself, the lack of evidence that change is occurring, the pain that may be associated with seeing our flaws, the sensibility of the steps, the person in charge of the process or who is going through the process with us all give rise to wanting to quit or circumvent the steps. It is through processes that we are able to see and measure growth in our lives. Each step clearly defined and laid out gives us a way to see progress and move with intentionality. How often have you felt like you were going in circles and found out later that you actually were just pushing the same dirt around because there were no defined tasks that needed to be completed to get you to your next phase, level or place in life? With no defined goals and no steps or process to get us there, we languish in no man's land hoping to hit a target, but we don't even know its location.

A process helps us define our responsibilities and create a step by step plan to establish how we are going to accomplish what we were created to do. It allows you to see gaps in the plan and then go get help to fill the gap or get skills so you can fill them. There is a scripture that says, "The steps of a good man are ordered by the Lord" (Proverbs 37:23). This seems to indicate that even God believes in a process and believes that good men and women follow processes to get to their intended purpose.

So those factor that make us want to give up suggest that our worth is just shy of the hard work it takes to push past those limitations. I submit that you are worth so much more. Each step you take to push past your pain, your boredom and your insecurities to stay the course is another affirmation that you are valuable and worth the effort. It is saying to yourself that you are worth fighting for. Stop letting trivial things hang you up. Stop letting hard circumstances be the reason you don't get that secondary degree, start that business, go after the promotion, buy that dream house, dare to love again after a broken heart. Life is too short and a well laid out plan that has been vetted by those who love you and care about your well-being is worth pursuing. Let the process work for you. Can I encourage you to stay the course and don't give up?

Okay I hear you talking in your head... "What happens if I don't see change?" Well, when you first start working out or go on a diet, you don't see immediate results. If you are like me, you actually gain weight first as muscle, because muscle builds first and weighs more than fat. This can be discouraging and tempt you to believe it is not working, causing you to want to give up. However, if you will stay the course, eventually the tide will turn and the progress will pick up rapidly. You may not see anything happen at first, but don't decide that nothing is working. Trust me when I say you are working on a six-pack under the surface because when the fluff is blown away, people will come running to ask of your wisdom.

For those who believe in God, you know that you can lean on Him. His word says "Trust in the Lord with all of your heart" (Proverbs 3:5). His process for our lives is good and He orders our steps in the direction that He intends us to go. If you put the work in, the change will happen and you will arrive at the desired end. It may not look like what you thought, but it will look like what God intended it to be. Faith, my friend, is required and a belief that you are worth the effort. This just in, I have a very special message for you: "You are more than worth it!" This is a promise - you and everyone else will see it if you just hang in there and work the process of transformation. It will work for you.

Intentional Blank Pages

Many of you reading have been in college and had that dreaded paper due the next day. Why you waited until the last minute, you have no idea. In fact, the last time you waited until the last minute you promised yourself that you would not do that again. And yet, here you are again sitting, staring at that blank page. Nothing is coming to your mind. All of your creativity has gone out the window. You don't know where to begin and all you know is you want it to be finished.

Maybe you have had to write a letter to someone to communicate something difficult and found yourself staring at the blank sheet not knowing what to say and, if you do, how it will be received. Go back to any of these moments. While you thought that your blank page days would end with college or that particular situation, you have discovered that blank pages follow us into our adulthood and into most phases of our lives.

Yes, of course I am using the phrase metaphorically, but sometimes it feels almost real - our life is nothing more than a blank page. Here are some examples of what I mean: you graduated from college and found that you have a degree but there are no jobs called Liberal Arts or any companies hiring anybody with the kinds of experience you have at the moment. "Hmmm, what do I do now..." Blank page. You married the person of your dreams but now, after giving them the last 20 years of your life, they say they have found a new love and you come home to an empty house, a dissolved marriage and a broken heart. You have to start your life over...

blank page. Perhaps you have worked for a company for 35 years, given them weekends, passed up opportunities to jump ship and now they have announced a new direction and you are staring at a layoff notice at 58 years of age and a blank page in life. This one is all too common: you put all your energy into the kids, everything you did was for them and now that the last one has left for college and barely calls home, you realize your whole identity was around those kids and you have no idea what you are going to do with your life now that being a mom or dad day in and day out is no longer required in this manner... blank page. Now staring at that blank page back in college or even in high school seems like a piece of cake, doesn't it?

Here is the good news: blank pages are opportunities for something amazingly new to be written on them. It means that something fresh, something that has never been in your life can now exist and that is exciting. The freedom and the liberty to step out and be what you have always dreamed to be is available when there is nothing in your way and that is what a blank sheet represents. This is the positive side of the equation if we can find the courage to see beyond the emptiness of it all. Most of our lives are so congested with stuff, people and busyness that when we have a clear path to change we hesitate because we are not accustomed to having the ability to really transform our lives. It almost seems too good to be true.

There is another aspect to this we must tackle and that is fear. A blank page in our lives is scary. What if we start out and we write the wrong script, what if nothing comes, what if our creativity is stifled and we cannot figure out what to do next?

What if it stays blank so long the ends of our pages curl up and the page turns that weird beige color? That is where the Creator of your incredible life and journey comes in. Jeremiah 29:11 says this: "'For I know I have the plans I have for you,' says the Lord, 'plans to prosper you and not to harm you to give you a future and a hope.'" There is already a plan for your life that was laid out before you were born. He knows the plan and did not trust it to anyone but Himself. There is nothing to fear. The plan is to prosper you and to give you an amazing future no matter what your past looks like, no matter what your current circumstances are, no matter how empty your life seems right now, there is hope and the possibilities are endless for life, love, happiness and joy. You have to believe that because it is true!

There is another perspective on this thought about the blank pages of life. Have you ever read a book and found that there is a blank page between chapters? Sometimes it may even have the words "This page intentionally left blank." When I was young, my godmother used to buy me books to read, the hardback kind that had that blank page before the next chapter started. I did not understand why that was there. As I grew older and went off to college, I found out that sometimes it was there to mark a hard stop from one chapter to another, to end the thought so that you could take note that the last chapter was completely over.

Our lives are sometimes like those books; they have blank pages between the chapters and seasons of our lives. It can be confusing as we move from one season to another when we don't know what is coming next and what we have is ending. It could be that this page has been intentionally left blank so that you could have a fresh start in life, so that what is old can be swept away and all things can be made new in you and around you.

Finally, the blank page may be there so that you can take a minute and ponder what happened in the last chapter or season of your life. What was the plot, what was the theme, what were you supposed to learn, what notes might you need to jot down about the last chapter and what lessons do you need to take into the next phase? You just may need that blank space to take a minute and breathe in nothingness before hurrying on to the next. It is okay take it. It is okay. We have to trust that the next chapter ahead will be there when we get to it and the story written is good and is moving towards a climactic ending. New characters may be added, the plot will continue to unfold, there may be suspense, there may be laughter, there may even be tears, but know that as people read your life, theirs will be enhanced. Don't be alarmed. I believe your life is going to be a page turner!

Fight for It!

I hope I am not putting words in your mouth, but I think I may have heard you say you are tired of fighting. You want to rest! Can I say I get it? I too am tired, tired of taking care of everybody, tired of working, tired of serving, tired of taking care of babies, my husband, my church, tired of fighting systems and systemic problems, tired of fighting because I am *not* a man, tired of fighting because I am a woman, tired of fighting to get the best education for my kids, tired of fighting for equality as African American. But can I tell you as I fight for social justice, religious freedom, equal rights and against human trafficking and so much more, I have finally come to realize that I have to fight to exercise self-care for me. It is imperative that I take care of myself with at least as much intentionality as I have for taking care of others. So often we are martyrs and think we are being noble in putting ourselves last. The problem with this line of thinking is that if we don't take care of ourselves, we won't be around to take care of anyone else.

The truth is, many of us let everything else take precedent over our own self-care and we think fighting for time for ourselves is selfish. We often start out wanting to serve those around us from a pure heart. However, over the course of time, we may get addicted to being needed and we can very easily move from serving out of a pure heart to serving with the expectation of getting the rush of knowing we are helping. It gets addictive. If not put in check, before long we are being run ragged taking care of anyone and everyone and our battery gets low. When we finally realize that our motives are not right, it is because we are so tired we want to throw it all away.

My friends, you have to let go of your past mistakes and fight for the great future you have inside of you. All of the things you have encountered up to this very moment have prepared you for this transformation moment. Fight through your anxiety and all the misperceptions about how you are not prepared. You are as prepared for change as you are going to be this very minute, period! Don't be intimidated by how big it seems. It won't all happen at one time. It will happen one moment at a time, day by day, and you can handle it. Your fight is mostly with your mind and that is why we started this whole transformation process with transforming your mind. You have to change it first to be ready for all the next steps. Your mind is ready. Each of us has to go to battle with our minds regarding how we see ourselves.

Next we step into the ring with our emotions to let them know we will not be controlled by them or how we feel from day to day. Transformation then comes to that climax where you have to have the discipline to make a decision with the full authority of your heart, your mind and your emotions. Decide that you are going to fight for what is rightfully yours because your Creator has already determined it to be before the foundations of the world were ever laid. You are not alone in this fight. All of heaven is rooting for you, those trusted voices are rooting for you, your circle of friends and family are there and God himself is rooting for you to be transformed into the person that you not only want to be, but were created to be.

Final note: make sure you are fighting the right battle. Never fight people. "For we fight not against flesh and blood…" it says in Ephesians 4:12. Don't make the battle against people. Those who fight against your transformation usually want you to stay the way you are, because in some way it must be convenient for them for you not to grow. Your growth will infringe upon their immaturity or cause you to stop enabling them or cause some kind of co-dependency to end. If this is the case, then it is high time change occurs and your transformation process will inevitably create the beginning of a transformation process in them. They too, by default, will have to change at least the part of their lives that included you staying in the same spot that you occupied in their life.

Destiny is calling you forward and you are answering. Don't let the sad faces, the heated arguments, and the manipulative tactics of those whose lives will be forced into a shift cause you to forego what is good for your life. I promise they will be ok and, in fact, they will be better because they will be forced to do what perhaps they should have done a long time ago. Fight for the independence to say no; it is liberating and it is often times straight from heaven itself.

So what are we going to do? We are going to fight to thrive, not just survive. We are not just fighting for the sake of fighting. We are locked in a battle for life and that more abundantly. So my friend, fight. Fight for your legacy, fight for your reputation, fight for your joy, fight for yourself. Fight to become the best you. There is a better you inside of you worth fighting for. A friend of mine, Brian Courtney Wilson has a song called "Worth Fighting For" and it

283

comes to mind as I write, even now. Yes, you are enough right now. This is true and if you never changed it would be good enough for most things.

Yet you and I both know that there is more in your tank: more gifts, more talent, more wisdom, more to give and to develop. So let's fight for the more that is in you to come out. Let's fight for the next chapter of your life that needs to be written. Let's fight for the story of your life to be written and told to those who need inspiration and a lifting up. Let's fight for the dream that you have had on the back burner. Let's fight for a change that may just be contagious enough to start a transformation revolution amongst those in your sphere of influence and cause those who see you to want to become a better version of themselves. Let's fight so that your children will know that they are worth fighting for. I fought to write this for you and I implore you to see that you are worth fighting for because your transformation is coming… in fact, it is here!

Connecting with Andrea

First of all, thank you for picking up *Transformed for Purpose* and taking the time to read it. If you don't already know, there is a corresponding **_free_** workbook that accompanies this book that you can receive on my website at www.andrea-humphrey.com. Over the past 20 years my focus has been on helping people transform their lives in a variety of capacities. As a life-coach to corporate executives and entertainment artists, I have walked many through seasons of change and powerful transitions. From owning a beauty shop to being president of a community development center, I have had the opportunity to talk to thousands of people who just needed help and wisdom on their next move in life. They needed someone to help guide them, point out pitfalls and encourage them that the seemingly impossible is actually doable and accessible.

My credentials from an educational perspective are an undergraduate degree in Economics and an MBA in Management. I am currently pursuing a Doctorate in Christian Education and Pastoral Leadership. I own and have owned several businesses, and I am the author of the book *More Than Just His Wife* available on Amazon, Barnes & Nobel and Kindle. But more than that my heart and passion is helping people live out their purpose. It seems I am really wired to *"help people get over the Hump"* in life and move on to their next!

If you are one who is in need of a coach who has experience in the academic world (I taught at a university for 12 years), the corporate world (The Walt Disney Company for 20 years) the entertainment industry (I have worked with various artists over the past 15 years, both secular and Christian), and in the religious realm (I have been pastoring for the past 15 years), then reach out and let's connect. Together we can move forward and see lasting transformation happen in your life. I am purposefully prepared and ready, how about you?

Transformation Specialist,

Andrea L. Humphrey, MBA

50921727R00163

Made in the USA
San Bernardino, CA
08 July 2017